BELT LINES

LEE BUTLER
BARDESS OF THE BELTLINE

ONION RIVER PRESS

Burlington, Vermont

Copyright © 2024 by Lee Butler

All rights reserved. No part of this publication may be reproduced, distributed, or transmitted in any form or by any means, including photocopying, recording, or other electronic or mechanical methods, without the prior written permission of the publisher, except in the case of brief quotations embodied in critical reviews and certain other noncommercial uses permitted by copyright law.

Onion River Press
Burlington, VT 05401
info@onionriverpress.com
www.onionriverpress.com

ISBN: 978-1-957184-63-0
Library of Congress Control Number: 2024911496

TABLE OF CONTENTS

Foreword	ix
My Phoenix City	1
Kudzu	2
Kate	3
Sky King	4
Dogs	5
Sort of Sonnet	6
Hostess and Rhino	7
The Finger	8
Read Aloud	9
Stoppings	10
Statues	11
Delta Divan	13
Markers	14
Hoboken	15
For My Father	16
Squadron of Crows	17
Blondie	18
Grateful Living	19
Two Fathers	20
I Mark You	21
Three Metal Figures	22
Nature's Sounds	23
Bike With Baseball Cards	24
Hobo	25
Frank	26
Laurel, Mary and Mallory	27
Mary and Larry	28
Tom	29
Power Lines	30
Three Blues	31
Why Don't You Drop Acid?	32
Azalea	33
Black and White	34
Capricorns	35
The Wave	37
Bennet	38
#755	39

"My Ex-Wife Was a Poet"	40
Dogs Love Poetry	41
Fred	43
Jerry	44
Sunflowers	45
Here	46
Adoration for a Child	47
Not Stopping	48
Vietnam Vet	49
All Hallows Eve	50
Olga, Trapeze Artist	51
Sorrow, Grief	52
Tom, Shane, Christopher Robin	53
Hawk	54
Silver Lines	55
Feather Duster Clouds	56
Elegy for a Tree	57
Valentines	58
Dandelions	59
Reed, Danny and Victoria	60
Month Names	61
The Island of the Spoken Word	63
Vandalism	64
Mr. Paul	65
Trash	66
Awkward April	67
Spider or Ladybug	68
My Exit	69
Witches	70
Reading Places	71
White Butterfly	72
4th of July Thank You	73
Victoria	74
Plato	75
Neal and Alex	77
Trumpet Vine	78
Grace	79
Four Monarchs	80
Joseph	81
Sarah and Nikko	82

Bruce and Isabel	83
Hope	84
Neal and Mike	85
Awe	86
Dancer	87
Drought	88
Janus	89
Bad Review	90
Lydia, Dearest Ray	91
Anna	92
Noon	93
February Passes	94
Unplugged Sounds	95
April Fools	96
Tiar's Ink	97
Hair	98
Dylan, Vivian	99
Clouds	100
Maypoles	101
Mother's Day	102
My Porch	103
Graduate	104
June	105
Hugs and Holds	106
Caldoon	107
Vivian	108
Sleuthing For Words	109
Dog Names	110
Hollis	111
We Need Water	112
Toasts	113
New Word	114
Lisa and Dimitri	115
Word Archaelogist	116
What Might Have Been Written	117
What's Next	118
Teachers	119
Jake the Dog	120
Grace, Not Miranda	121
Glen	122

Penumbra	123
GG	124
Bird Builders	125
Manhole Covers	126
Small Gifts	127
Donna	128
Cellular Listeners	129
Lori	130
Atoms of Thanks	131
Worms – Robin Heaven	132
Matthew and Tim	133
Morphing Reality	134
Daylight Savings Time	135
Volleyball Ken	136
Mothers and Children	137
Stop and Hear Roses	138
Repurposed Materials	139
Rome	140
Noises	141
Farmers and Poets	142
Unnamed	143
Dan	144
A Sleeve of Poem #133	145
Bride and Groom	146
Being Bitten	147
Dogs as Assistants	148
Swallowtail	149
Spy Novel	150
#2 Pencil	151
Autumn	152
Gecko	153
O'Clock Time	154
My Theater	155
Octoberfest	156
Robyne and Cliff	157
Untoward	158
Leave-taking	159
Adieu	160

TO MY MOTHER, FAYE EVANS BUTLER, WHO TAUGHT ME THAT EACH WORD IS IMPORTANT.

TO MY HUSBAND, RAY PELOSI, WHO INTRODUCED ME TO THE BELTLINE.

AND, TO MY BELTLINE LISTENERS, WHO BECAME MY MUSES.

FOREWORD

It all began with an outstretched obsidian glass hand blown by my daughter-in-law, Kate. The artist had stealthily affixed it—as a guerrilla installation—to a tree on the Eastside Trail of the Atlanta Beltline, the 22-mile-long loop path tracing an old railroad corridor, even though only "official" artwork was sanctioned for placement on the trail. One day, at the invitation of Kate and her husband, Ray's son, Matt, Lee and I decided to have a look at it.

While we were there, Lee noticed what a splendidly unique venue the Beltline was, so she and I began walking the trail every weekend, down and back, to get the full Beltline experience. After several months of this, Lee got the notion to honor that experience in a series of 155 poems—one more than the number of Shakespeare's sonnets—and read each new poem to Beltline passersby every Saturday, weather permitting, for the next five years—right across the way from that tree with the glass hand. Whoever stopped to listen got a free copy of the poem on ecru card stock.

Celebrated as the Bardess of the Beltline in Atlanta-area media and by the legion of friends and admirers she met along the trail, Lee is offering the fruits of that special time in her life to you, in this book.

—Ray Pelosi, March 2024

MY PHOENIX CITY

Gathering the girth of my phoenix city,
breadths and lengths convey themselves on
the concrete path with wheels, feet, and blades.
Their shirts declare beliefs, attitudes,
their bottoms show wiggle, angles.
Some are so wired up they do not mark
bicycle bells, huffing dogs or runner's pace.
The sentinels admonish the loud, fast and littering.
The Couples caught on each other's fingertips or
walking adjacent, breathe in unison.
The Ones keep pace with selves,
sunglasses obscuring their gathering thoughts.
The Trios and Quintets flow, step, bump,
the second and third vying for position.
The String of Tourists, fingers pointing
questioning, oohing, aching while I silently agree.
I reach Irwin,
a revolution around the yellow guidepost,
my Boyfriend and I head back to our Monroe beginning.

KUDZU

Kudzu, not unlike the stone walls of Scotland
twiggy braids curling up and around the hillside
winding nature's Severan Wall
holding the line of earth in place.

Some have crashed the plastic gates
as evidenced by the trampled webs.
A breech in the barrier
which leaves unchecked footsteps dominating
the delicate grasses.

An allowed opening, leading to the rusted Corinthian.
Should I bring unnatural homage in the form of
a bouquet from a nearby warehouse grocery?
Who is honored, a long ago engineer?

New construction, green insulation
each week closer to the finished date.
Who will live behind the promise
of the uncompleted stacked vistas
which are fenced in to deter theft of supplies?

A grey incline of painted panels,
A concrete magic carpet
The only deterrent is the height.
The child at the top did not look back as he ascended,
but now is frightened as he looks into the canyon
without a net to break his fall.

"Might I join you next week if I bring something sweet?"
A request I do not yell, but think
when I see the Father and two children ensconced on high
in their escalated Adirondacks.
Instead … We cautiously make our way down
a worn unofficial path to the backside
of a brick patio where just inside the gate
our tapas await.

KATE

Kate, the artistic warrior
executes her guerrilla installation.
The walled overpass is impenetrable,
so her drill finds a pine
which will bear the screws
to hold "Spreading the Love".
Her generation does not wait for galleries.
Gloriously, the tree bark becomes the museum wall.
Her obsidian glass combined with Apollo
create nature's chiaroscuro.
A sense of volume made with sand and sun.
Observant strollers saw the piece,
paused to reflect on the proffering palm
and outstretched chin.
Without guards to prevent theft,
someone stole it;
A private collector, I hope.

SKY KING

A commando skater in camouflage, a do-rag in place of the green beret
is he late for battle?
Fisted, thumbs up pumping the air.
What's in his backpack?
Is he reconnoitering
or delivering treats to his squadron of pets?

A bicycle built for two, mother and son
his rubber tipped sneakers are not co-piloting.
He is a scofflaw, letting Mom do all the heavy forwarding.
Can he hear her as she speaks to the air in front?
Are her words captured in a comic bubble over her head
so that he may read them?

A cartoon teenager, cap on backward
dancing on his wooden ballroom
using every inch of the mural skateboard
like the ice dancers use the four corners of the rink.
Lithe footwork, but gangly flopping arms
which belong to a drunken tightrope walker.

The pink Airflow Sky King, circa 1950
is on display for me to covet
I am too big for the sparkle streamers
I'd attach to the handlebars.
I'm peddling so fast my mane flies behind me.
My lace edged socks flurry as plaited tails.
I gallop off down the expanse near Ponce.

DOGS

Water and canopies in Paris – no French poodle but two dog-dogs
(My grandmother's term for indiscriminate breeds).
Lots of Ladies, but no Tramps as there are leash laws and dogs know.

Stainless steel bowls with Bocce nearby,
the player's pooches yawn in the shade
as the leagues moan, shout and sweat.

Picnic tables provide menus of leftovers
Bits are brushed off for the quick birds.
The PAWS couple strut with Gertrude
hoping to assist in her adoption.
Tiny toes tipping and tapping trying to keep up
with neon fleeted masters.

A Lhasa Apso curled in the front basket while her mistress
pedals with brightly painted and golden-ringed bare feet.
Does she provide Tibetan bottled water for her Dolly Canine?

There aren't many who are allowed to mosey or lollygag.
No stopping and standing (clock conscious owners).
A matching couple with mismatched dogs
Stop to listen.
After they've left
there is a pile from the bigger dog
left on the pebbled rug.
I anthropomorphize, "It's not my fault he didn't pick up after me."

SORT OF SONNET

"Please write at least one rhyming verse for me."
Granting your request, a simple sonnet,
no tankas or haikus, I quite agree,
For Faye, a fourteen line metered banquet.
Your daily trip, a mile and a quarter,
a spring action rubber tipped skiing pole
securing balance, it doesn't falter.
Your daughter's firm arm will assist your stroll
when sauntering Beltline at leisured pace.
Describing the fauna, flora and art
rays and breezes lightly touching your face.
Missing nothing, sight is not always smart.
"The seeing see little," Miss Keller said,
and with the other four you'll be fully fed.

HOSTESS AND RHINO

Dance easing in and out among the parties
her black lace dress
flowing with her in between the tables.
Breezy-easy verbal skilled
welcoming efficiency.
Our place now that we are recognized.
The figs and chorizo have been anticipated
I want to write a review,
but…
How do I use letters to sing a chorus of yums?
A woozy return walk
After a pitcher of sangria
past a shiny rhino
back to our side street parked steed.

THE FINGER

Dear Sir,

Why did you give me the finger?
You made an effort to turn around and gesticulate.
Your vigorous topless form was not running full force.
It was a conscience decision,
the third of your phalanges erected to distinguish your meaning.

What was an affront to you?
Did the timbre of my voice
or my comment that everyone has " the soul of a poet"
remind you of an offense you were unable to address?
Perhaps it was meant for a boss, an acquaintance or idea
that you wished to flip off.
Was it Beltline Rage?

Thank you for your middle digit
as it came up near the end of my weekly recitation
and gave me another topic for a poem.

READ ALOUD

The grey couple leans over the mosaic overpass
looking into the North Avenue canyon.
"Would you like to hear my poem about the Beltline?'
Her Stop Sign palm
along with an emphatic, "I'm tired!"

A man with magazine-cover-worthy hair states,
"What are you complaining about?"
I give my barker spiel.
"I'm a retiring English teacher,
I write poems about the Beltline,
They are not for sale nor are they religious or political,
I would just like to read it to you."
Sometimes I add a codicil, "Everyone has the soul of a poet."
With him I leave the footnote out.
"I don't want you to read it to me."
He take the offered paper, folds it neatly
and places it inside his fashionable jacket.
"I'll read it myself, later,"
Did he?

Many rushed
Focused upon getting "it" done.
Workout, Work, List Making, Pondering.
Treading words on their devices.
Why do some feel they must lie? and say,
"I'll stop on my way back."
Do they wish to not hurt a stranger's feelings?
One in twenty offer me money.
A homeless man ignores me as he is ignored.

A lovely mead-colored pony-tailed lass
explains me to an unrelated group that gathers
I want to reach out and squeeze her in thanks.
The collective nods,
courtesy and civility live.

STOPPINGS

Stoppings

A baseball cap and cloche
Elbows on the ledge

Under the oak
Huffing ribs beneath the T-shirt

Tying the untied
Two loops into a bow

Leaning against the bike rack
Stretching hamstrings like pliers

Hand clutching hand
Turning toward to whisper then kiss

An unplanned trip
Falling caused by an unseen stone

Skateboarder jumps overboard
Walking away, leaving his ship as a stumbling block

Bent over picking up a litterer's leftovers
No receptacle except her purse

Waiting until the others in the caravan of wheels
Catch up

Pausing for a breeze
to brush closed eyelids

Wanting to stop and listen to the poet
But...
"I'm late for fill in the blank."

STATUES

The trio of rail workers
skeletons of hard labor
The middle one's movement
hindered by a child curling inside his ribs.
Ghost train's chords steam behind the track they laid.

Skyline cyclists
The willowy female seems to have the lead
but, it is a gust of wind that arbitrarily thrusts her wheels forward
winnowing out
the other riderless tires that
singularly roll atop the meadow grasses

Just the countenance of the rhino
Did he lose his body as an earthmover for the Beltline?
A silent snort
A headless body charging nowhere
chasing scents from nearby restaurants

I want to plant climbing vines
at the base of the sun and orange phoenix
but, that would turn the hollow bird
into a hallowed hall of ivy
mixing earth with air
and the wings could not fire up
being earth bound.

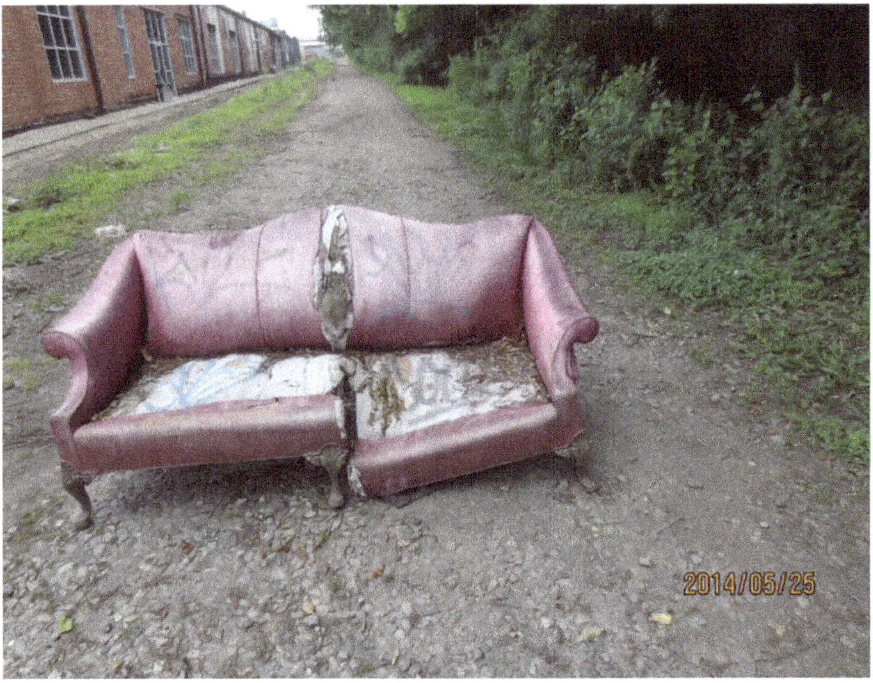
2014/05/25

DELTA DIVAN

Delta Divan, a faded couch
Glorious parlor days gone by
Faded mauve rose embossed silk
Your posture was once erect and graceful
Now you are missing one of your carved claw feet
and are propped up by a cement block
Gracing the space between loft advertisement
and steam grates.
Discarded just beyond Irwin resting
on a carpet of packed clay.
You are on nature's veranda.
No one to dust the vagrant leaves which have fallen
into your lap.
No Beaux seated on your graffitied cushions.
Did you have lacy antimacassars
before the spider's webs hung between your arms?
I frame you,
Click you,
imagining your original rotogravure.

MARKERS

Scrap plywood words hung by wire to the webbing
Were the dangling nouns chosen by children?
My pinkie wrapped around yours
as you keep me on the inside
as did the gentlemen on the city sidewalks of yore
The Post Oak which needs a yellow ribbon round its middle
Your refrain each week, "The distance seems shorter."
My response, "because we know the route and what comes next."
The nearly summer nineties refreshed by breezes that arrive
Just before we get too hot.
Reaching the underpass
refrigerated by the dark concrete and gurgles of water.
Tiny varieties and variations of vibrations above our heads
as we breathe the cool.
The chocolate mulch mounded up
used as a bench by a runner and his panting Bulldog.
Holding hands homeward
we step off the path
and encounter
two plastic soldiers placed atop a mailbox
posed by a grown-up child
a tiny duel in our Sunday landscape.

HOBOKEN

Have you been to Hoboken?
Do the children react to all the gapped teeth figures,
the pastels reminiscent of their infant bassinets?
The enormous creepy carrots that cartoons crave,
but kids hide on their plates.
"Where's the duck, where's the duck?", a father questions
A properly helmeted redhead points and screeches,
"There it is, There it is,"
"You are so Smart, You are so Smart."
Her head remains tilted up toward the duck.
Has he read her Dr. Seuss?
Years hence will her memories be flooded with
underpass murals she bicycled by?
Will she dream of New Jersey and wonder why?

FOR MY FATHER

"Bob" the sign said.
Nearby the bicycles sleep and the rooster crows
A mountain biker and hiker,
my father would have mircroscoped the urban path.

The errant wildflowers unwilling to be fenced, pouring under
Varieties which thirst for water forced out by the hearty
One ruff of lace in a field of black eyes
All of Susans, ladies-in-waiting for Queen Anne.
He would have read Latin stones, noting the indigenous.

"Rules are for when brains run out",
but being a civil civilized man,
he'd have adhered to the right hand rules.
The admonitions of my Sierra childhood traipses
"Take everything out that you bring in",
charge me to pick up the careless cans.
I resist thanking the two men ahead
eating their way up the Line
who return litter to the plastic take out they have carried in.

Birds dancing dominance
Swiping intruders with feathered swords
Piping tweets and whistling warnings
Perhaps Bob would have stopped the over-wired,
"See something besides texts and hear nature's talk."

SQUADRON OF CROWS

A squadron of crows on their ratty black boards
fly down the sidewalk in a far flung formation.
A father and son unicycle team pull off to the side
waiting for traffic to subside.
The father anticipates a hole in the flight pattern
before he silently motions to his son to merge in.
The fledgling hesitates
another jerking head signal from father
and they are away.
Watching the take-off,
I have failed to notice a jump-off landing.
Where is his ship?
His shoed feet don't have wings
No motors allowed on the Beltline.
In his palms, two metal plates each with one steel wheel.
It is Ryan and his free lines.
Two skate squares without laces.
His injured friend, Slade
sidelined on a slim twelve speed.

BLONDIE

"I'm famous," she said.
"I'm not," I replied.
"Do you get tired of fame?", I asked.
"Sometimes it's hard, they made a film about me.
I'm Blondie."
"I was featured in a Cub Foods commercial,
they went into bankruptcy."
She offered me money for my poem, I declined.
"It's a gift, it is my passion."
"You're sweet, this is sweet. Thank you, I'll keep it."
Her stage name is a cookie, a comic and a band.
"What's your real name?"
"Anita."
You are Grace in Hebrew and Italian
and an Iranian water goddess.
You were right, everyone knows who you are.
Thank you, Anita, for being my first famous listener.

GRATEFUL LIVING

Are you Grateful Living.
Separated @ death from Jerry?
No life nor spring in your step
Trudge your begrudging feet moving forward
Your glassed face straight ahead
Each week Thrice
Twice you pass me in my place
Once, on Sunday when I join the walkers without reciting
I think maybe I'll wave and say "Hey" Southern style.
I was afraid you'd groan, "Hey get outta my way."
Did you change direction, time and place?
I missed my chance to catch you off guard.
You've stopped walking by.

TWO FATHERS

Father has her bicycle over his shoulder
Sagging behind as she sprints ahead
He shifts his burden to his left
so he may hear his companion chatter sport scores.
His Fast Forward daughter reaches
an imaginary finish line crack in the walk
and turns around to wait for the Languisher.

A chastising father, "Get up, you're not hurt."
Growling at the six year old cyclist for crying
I want to intervene,
Claw him for ruining fun and fancy.
The sky is sinking for the crestfallen child.

Next moment, a Dad scooping up a tutu-ed toddler.
He throws her cloudward shouting, "Yippee."
She forgets she has fallen
as he tosses her again into the springy sky.

I MARK YOU

We are all Homo Sapiens
Some with canines in tow
Our found bones would forensically indicate we are the same
We are all on the Beltline, so we have the same sense of direction.

I wanted someone to mark you, notice you, see you.
I'm it.
Not a politician tallying your handshake
Nor a chaplain counting your soul
Some oligists believe it is language that differentiates us.

Many of you give thumbs up, some smile
Few, a bob of the head
Frequently, elucidators, "Can't Stop."
I understand Alice's Rabbit, "Late."

Week 13 was lucky
Ricky said, "I love your spiel: you made me smile every time I passed you.
I had to stop this week.
You are my new favorite person."

THREE METAL FIGURES

Three metal figures have come to gaze. To reflect?
or to be reflected upon?
This happens in a fortnight.
The squatters move in, possession is 9/10ths.
A passer-by has draped one of the heads with a cloth
Trash has gathered from around their feet.
Hikers ignore them as they do me
Bikers want neither literature nor art
Use their forms as a place to lean the spokes
One walker gives the middle figure's head an officious pat.
I try some pitter but the patter waves me off.
I'm live, but it doesn't matter.
I'll bring my broom and dustpan to clean between us
The three deserve tidy pedestals.
I must find the muralist who painted the back drop.
I will ask him to restore Lord Byron's signature
it has faded.
Ok, It's not Westminster, but it is this poet's corner.

NATURE'S SOUNDS

No rap needles scraping the vinyl
No steel drum's percussive roar
No jazzman's wooden stick riff
Nor an oboist's breath through the reed
No drummer brushing his snare
No wanded triangle's dinner bell
No conductor flicking her stick   **BUT,**
Bird's rapacious refrains recorded **Pre-Pliocene**
Clapping of brown magnolia leaves for the wind
Wheezing of dried blooms releasing their seeds
Wings of the blue-jays flapping in flight fights
The hum of dust blown up in a breeze
The silent sprinting stratus clouds
Does the poet's voice register?

BIKE WITH BASEBALL CARDS

The Youngster's baseball cards and clothespins sing
in the spokes
I wish to have a phone of two tin cans and twine
So we can speak about the past.
His spider handlebars have rubber grips
and multicolored streamers.
Mine was pink metallic hung with a white wicker basket.
He has a matching shouldered parrot that does not wing away.
I had a teal parakeet whose careless keeper
left the cage door open.
He has stopped to listen.
"I'm going to hang this up when I get home."
I hope it's on his fridge with crayoned maps
and a magnet collection.

HOBO

The hobo shouldering his bindle
Not a bum or a tramp, but an itinerant worker
Using Hoboglyphs (sociologist's word not theirs')
illiterate, but able to communicate thru drawings.
The English 26 are nothing more than symbols
Leaving messages for their peers.
00 connected, was encouragement, don't give up
a cat's face signifying the home of a kind lady,
where you might get a free meal.
Hoho code, texts for fellow travelers
No ink, nor paper, but coal chalk and fence posts.
/// scrawled warned, "Unsafe"
Icons for food, shelter and fellowship left by the like minded
Does the HOBOE sprayed on the cement block
mark the grave of one who rode the rails?

FRANK

He is Frank, so… I ask him
"Why don't people stop to listen?"
"Fear," he supposes.
His children said that he does not speak English well.
I disagree
He asks,
"Where do you get your great words?
Each of your poems has words that fit."
He is gone for five weeks,
but now he is back and Miami brown.
He is now regular at my overpass and I serve him up words.
Frankly, I had missed his accented sincerity.
Last week I saw him out of context.
I was a walker going in the opposite direction.
I spied him and crossed to greet him
Nearly colliding with a helmeted gladiator.
"My bad, My mistake, I'm sorry" I called to the air.
He caught me in my imbalance and righted me,
Carefully.

LAUREL, MARY AND MALLORY

Three with drippy sticks of frozen syrup
Berry flavors licked by Cinnamon, Clove and Anise
Their variety of browns accented by neon printed shorts
and oval, round and square shaped shades.
Giggly girls with eager grins
Laughing behind their palms
Safety in numbers for stopping
Unison sighs, trio of "Ahhs" when introduced to my boyfriend
Laurel, Mary and Mallory
Little Black Tee-shirted three
The one who is familiar with me
Does a verse of introductions ending with Lee

MARY AND LARRY

Mary and Larry's first time
Thank you for letting me introduce you to Atlanta's alley
Mary's childlike thrills and Larry's observant skills
I want them to like my discovery
I'm invested I don't wish to disappoint
Have I built it up too much?
Did I choose my investors wisely?
Wanting them to see the Big Deal
The Crackers' magnolia outfield catches the fan's eye
Mary's irises are attracted by the coneflower's pink

TOM

Weekday mover of dirt is perched atop its pile of work
Its silence is yellow
Hung from its arm a pale blue Chinese paper lantern
A small gem dazzling in a weak breeze
I am not the only one who sees it
A tidy photographer parks his bike and stalks the image
Moving himself as an instrument
Not a selfie taker
He asks, "What are you about?"
He wants to click me reading.
I perform. Did he capture the recitation?
Poems are movement across the page and out of my mouth.
He took stills not moving pictures.
I use words, he uses exposures.
Did he get me?
I got him.

POWER LINES

Power lines send forth light and possibility for all the mechanics of life
Birds build their nests with leftovers, but choose to hang out on wires.
Certain species choose branches as the humans lease their lofts.
Have we forgotten natural nature?
attempting to spark Pre Cambrian
responses before fire.
Beneath the Beltline lie the remains and beginnings of time
All the elements needed for creation
except thought, which is not on the periodic chart.
Beyond the wood pulp that makes this paper,
is now the Cloud where the images are stored.
Have the Angels been relocated
to make room for the filing cabinets?

THREE BLUES

Your three tiered dress Sky, Royal, Navy
is invited to listen to my poem by your Royal tee father
"That's not a poem, it doesn't rhyme."
Your five year old stance
Your stare-severe critical glance
You are waiting giving me a chance
To make those last words end in a dance.
You are leaning on one of the North Avenue Trio
You move on, no time for adults who don't know what poems are
There is a tree across the way that knows what limbs are for
Father waits for me to finish
I tell him, it happens all the time
Children want rhyme.

WHY DON'T YOU DROP ACID?

Your drive by bicycle editorial:
"Why don't you drop some acid?"
Acid is a caustic combination of chemicals
That has altered the patterns of the spider's web
You did not stop to listen,
So I will not accept your criticism of my lines
Just a careless comment on my form filling the space,
Not the form of my words on the page or in the air
I cannot give credence to your negative,
unlike the editor of a magazine who rejected my verse.
Jean Sibelius said it best,
"A statue has never been erected in honor of a critic."

AZALEA

Three colors of asters: white yellow and lavender
Three colors of morning glories: white blue and rose
Fall flowers on the Beltline
No Azaleas until now
Her mother studies opera
The landscape enhanced by her head nestled in her father's cleft
No squirming, no shouting, she is secure in his curve.
Her sleep is a song of satisfaction
Unlike the soon faded bushes of first spring
This blossom will grow to grandeur
Making her parents' garden glow with first words,
First walks, first sentences and first runs.
I will remember her as the introduction to a new species.

BLACK AND WHITE

Grey and Beige
Elegant, Short
As they walk away, I thought
Why didn't I tell them they are the Most?
I want to photograph with words
Black and White, not color. That's what the serious artists use.
Round professor glasses in jewel tones, sapphire and ruby
Bowl haircuts with subtle highlights
Standing Links
They'd win a three legged race
Grace in their leisurely saunter
They are new to the Beltline and I'm glad to be the greeter.
I'm the arrow on the mall map "You are here".

CAPRICORNS

Capricorns
There are two types: the ones on the mountain top
and this one in the valley
Alone and munching the mulch
or captured and colluding with the herd.
Your reign begins on the first day of winter
And
You rule longer than any other sign
You are friends with Pan
Independent, climbing higher away from the group.
Smallest constellation in the Zodiac, only 414 square degrees
Old Year, New Year, Here at the end, sighted at the beginning
A child climbs upon your crippled leg,
The Tribe has moved on.
I will be looking for Aquarius and his water jugs
to take your place.

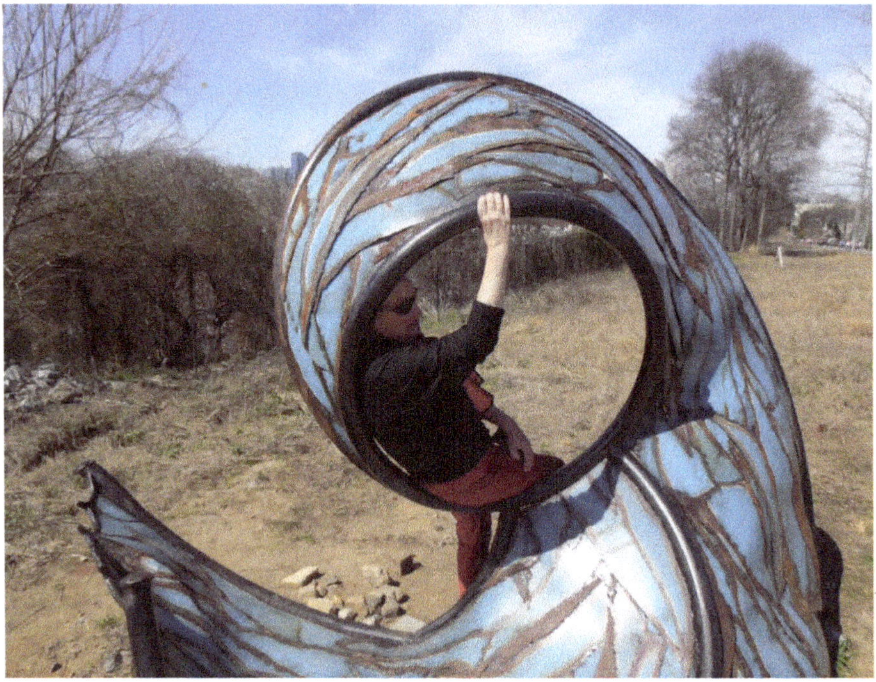

THE WAVE

In the waving grasses with their foam tassels
Rises an enormous castle of a Wave.
A royal crest, a ship of metal water
A curl that I am caught in as I sail away to Beltline shores.
Nature's pipeline catches the surfers and dashes them
Here toddlers can crawl along the curves
and nap in the sound of the wind thru its tunnels
A rolling ribbon of steel
Perfect for snorkeling
Amongst the sedges and weeds
where I will find treasure,
a rare word.

BENNET

After I learn his name, Bennet,
My prejudice thinks he belongs in a pram
Not an ergonomic stroller
No need to bend over to consider his perfectly round face
tucked against a pale blue animal.

Two toddlers seated side by side
in a figure eight parlor settee on wheels
Flirting, Courting?
Being pushed at a feverish pace.
Will there be time to stop
for sundaes topped with stemmed cherries?

Dangling legs, like charms on a necklace
emerge from the front-pack papoose.
Mama cups her cellphone in one hand
and the baby's bottom in the other.
Her pace quickens after "Gotta Go"
and a sniff of her palm.

#755

There was nothing on stage but grasses and insects
The painted backdrop of stylus clouds and various blues
Each week saw horses, bricks, boards and paint arrived.
A multi-leveled proscenium arch was constructed
The power tool hands danced a chorus
including Sunday matinees.
Drilling, Sanding, Spraying Beltline acrobats
a Flurrious production, that show has closed.
Balcony seat #755 can see me now,
but without a mike they cannot hear me.
Roommates from the Grand Tier descend to listen.
Acoustics of overhead planes
and alleyway emergency vehicles
cancel out my weekly recitations.
All of my patrons must have front row center standing.

"MY EX-WIFE WAS A POET"

My invitation is extended across the stones.
Many RSVP, "On my way back I'll stop."
"No, my ex-wife was a poet."
His declination is firm with an exclamation point.
The red cork-screwed curls hesitated
She turned to gaze, but felt inclined to stay with the group
Again, she turned around, but could not release their grasp.
"It's hot, I'd stop, but it's too HOT."
It is summer in Atlanta.
"I'm scoping for a brew."
I can offer cool words and the shade of a parasol
A two minute party and an introduction to a stranger
Your thank you note is listening to my verse.

DOGS LOVE POETRY

The hors d'oeuvre dog dotting and dashing his way along,
his Morse Code does not keep up with his brother, the hound
using ten notes for everyone of the big dog's song.
The red strapped Bassett's leash slaps muted sound
whilst the Chow's invisible fishing line strains the master's wrist.
A strong gust could soar him into a furry balloon.
Neither dog concerned with its collared walk twist
but, owner is entangled with headset/step counter tunes.
Dogs want water and relieving stops.
I call out, "Dogs love poetry, a scientific fact."
The canines strain at their humans, wanting to drop
the pretense of a route. They careen toward my act,
but his reaction to their veering off course is terse.
He cannot tolerate their predilection for verse.

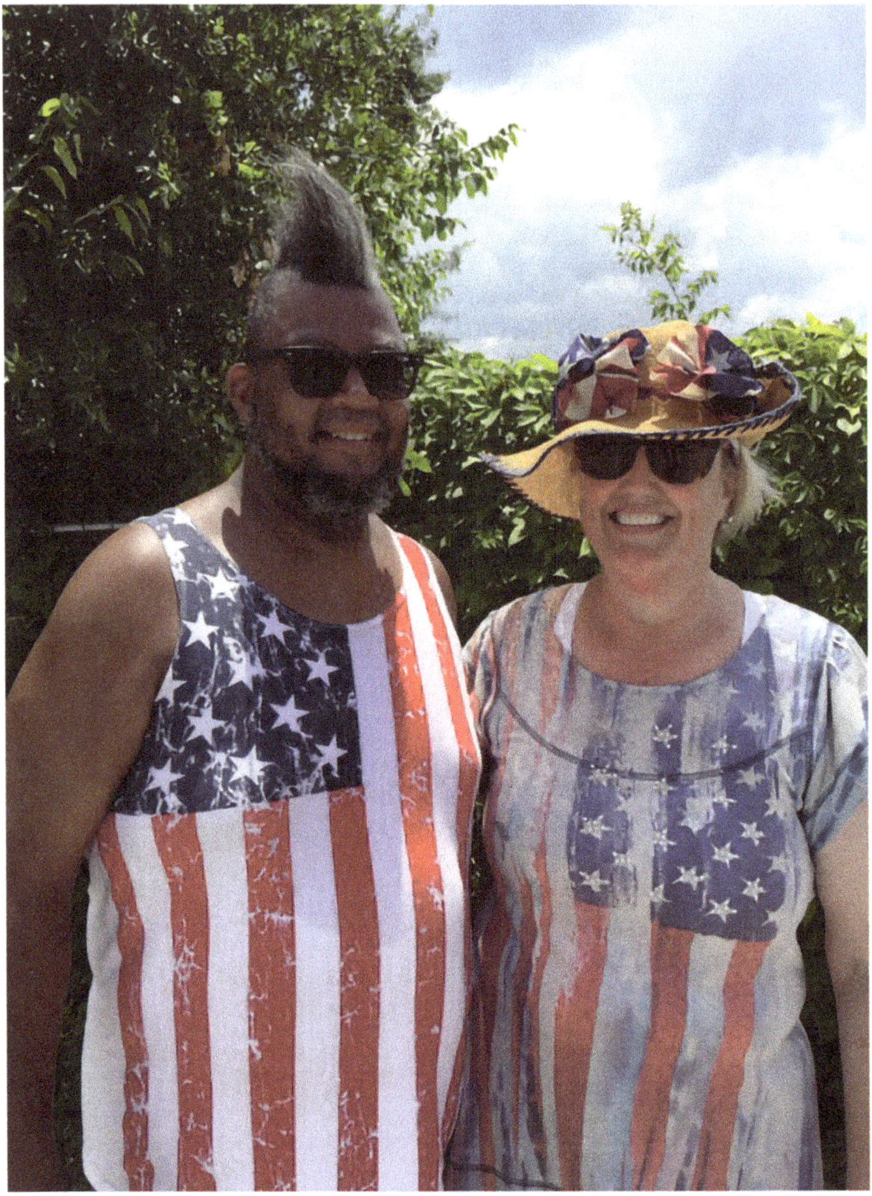

FRED

Fred with his Hermes stride
His sneakers take his message of invigoration up the path.
No name brand Adonis,
no t-shirt declaring his viewpoints
He will turn around at some point
and come back to collect this week's poem.
His Mohawk coif rising up as an exclamation point
a cadence of swift courtesy
His journey is one for sport,
But his stretches include the stopping to listen.

JERRY

Saturday Luncher, Jerry
Baby Boomer, drinker of hefty cocktails
Ash hair inherited from his ad-man father?
He's a stroller. If parking's not handy he will not hike.
Enthusiastically, "I'll come every week and bring friends.
You'll be the post luncheon entertainment."
He doesn't, he doesn't disappoint.
I was one week's distraction,
not a Saturday commitment,
a poetical bite, not an epic banquet.
His choice for dining has been serving for 87 years,
An Atlanta institution.
I'm new, a 16 month landscape recitation.

SUNFLOWERS

Black backpack, t-shirt, bicycle sped by
Big faced sunflowers flowed out of the opening
I shouted out about the rays
captured by the yellow saucers' contrast.
Marty turned around, peddling back with his blooms.
His turn was desire to tell me about a winning back.
Ivy had called it off.
Delving,"Will these cheery blossoms turn her face back toward him?"
"No, I am torturing myself with an excuse to see her."
Hope does spring
If I were she, I'd consider these multi-seeded heads
a daring gesture of rejection and at least incline my eye.
Her green name is fresh loyalty.
My silent prayer follows him on his way,
"Give him another try."

HERE

Detroit, New York, and San Francisco round the corner toward home
Caps on their fans forward, sideward and backward, no chalk line.
Rastafarian dreadlocks tucked into a knit cap, taking deep breaths
Is it Marley or Mendelssohn marching him up the aisle?
Doctor in theater blues hat deep throatily recording
Oxford accent into his device No visible blood,
his rubber tipped necklace swings in time to his step
Dark suited man running more than four cubits
He knows the Divine presence is always overhead,
Hence the yarmulke dome.
A Bubby's square rolled into a headband, keeps sweat off
the lithe sprinter's face.
Fingertips digging forward in the heavy air, she brushes me a wave
A Gold wheat wide brim stops to hear.
Her clean house on the prairie face shaded from glare
Last listener for the day, her husband's advice sent her … Here.

ADORATION FOR A CHILD

Four generations form a semi-circle audience
At 180 degrees are piercing black eyes with white awnings
Great silent presence she responds to Grand's voice,
"Listen, we are stopping to hear her."
Without sound she moves into position.

Baby with a slick of bright copper hair
plumply seated in a nest of white
I wish I could be familiar and bend to smell the sweetness
and pet the locks
transfixed by the beginning
all of my attention is taken by the translucent putti's skin
no words, just the purity go a smile without teeth

a hemisphere of woman
brought in by a claim
I long to delight and charm
and earn their lauds.

I read the words
The daughter collects the proof
Thanks me for the poem
and the adoration of the child.

NOT STOPPING

Shouldering a case of beer, whistling a cheerful accompaniment
Striding toward the party, "Gotta get there while the brew's cold."

Little brown bags with twine handles, one at the end of each arm
held by forefinger and thumb, She's a tightrope walker
Stopping to add my words to her load would topple the shopper.

Surveying? Clip board tucked under, which boxes will he check?
Guessing his to-do list does not include listening to a poet
He gates away, willfully not looking in my direction.

Dragging deflating balloons and a limp duffle bag
While clutching a five-year-old's post birthday-caked hand
She lifts her head to acknowledge me.
He's sticky and worn out, so is she, but
"Next time I'll stop."
"Me too," says he.

VIETNAM VET

Worn sand camouflage younger than Vietnam
sagging wraith, clean and polite
Beige desert, sloping tired
His approach is slow and deliberate.

Don't be afraid of me." / " I'm not, should I be?"
"I won't harm you." / "I am not expecting you to."
"What are you doing here?" / " I am a poet."
"I don't have any money." / "My poems are free."

"Sometimes I sleep in the dog park
Sometimes I get work at the garden store
Sometimes people give me food they have bought just for me
Sometimes the cops come by and ask us to leave.
Sometimes I don't want to move."

"Last winter a man paid for three nights in a hotel.
He didn't want anything.
I'd like to thank him.
He kept me from freezing to death.
My name is Ray
I'll fold your poem and put it in my pocket."

There but for the Grace _____
You know the rest.

ALL HALLOWS EVE

Costumes, silver and gold spandex
muscles winking in the wrinkles of fabric
striding down Atlanta's concrete runway
Dogs as a fashion accessory, ruffs round their necks
prancing at the ball
barking with delight

Revelers masked in shades
haunting the gyms during the week
peddling gravestones on recumbent bikes
You have come to reveal your masqueraded selves
on this sunny All Hallows Eve.

Will you offer a treat for my turn of phrase?
I imagine pleasing you and receiving
A wax lip smile
A Lady Finger high five
An apple of your eye-bobbing head approval

Will I be the jester and make the King laugh?

October 31, 2015

OLGA, TRAPEZE ARTIST

She swings her slim leg over the bar to stop
Her near topple alarms me to catch her
She doesn't need a spotter, She kicks the stand
and leans against the wheels to listen.
She is a trapeze artist without a place to practice.
She's come to Atlanta to Engineer a Masters
No Ramblin' Wreck, no rather dainty-strength ascending a rope
to grasp the bar and fast float across North Avenue.
She'll release, catch hold of another
jungle-gyming all the way back to campus.
Olga, clad in black and gold honoring the first flyer, Jules Leotard
She'll graduate, return to New York and perform her structural feats.
Salutes and Pirouettes, skyscrapers without catchers
Her cable of diagrams drafting new combinations.

SORROW, GRIEF

"Have you ever written about grief?"
Two slight Ladies
The question coming from the striped scarf.
"I ask because my husband died and my friend,"
She cupped the other's shoulder,
"just lost her husband."
"Oh, I wish you hadn't said anything."

I share my losses, Father and Grandmother.
"They are not lost."
She lets me hear her sorrow.
Her friend retrieves an anonymous poem from her pocket.
She recites it and they discuss it.
I clasp her hands as she receives her tears.
There will be more to come,
But what comfort in walking with a friend
In easy discomfort
Relaxing with an ache.
The Beltline, a passage for mourning.

TOM, SHANE, CHRISTOPHER ROBIN

Recorder Tom, always from the left
A capped head, zinc oxide nose and limboing gait.
After my recitation, discussions of other art forms
He is embracing jewelry making
I'm hoping his peacock will make an appearance
in Sterling not Gold.

Clicking Shane approaching with lens
The jingle bells of old fashioned cameras
Rapid snapping popcorn pictures hanging on a line in dark room
No selfie stick nor tripod, but a neck strapped aperture.
"Now, one shot without a smile."
I manage to quell, but my teeth rebel
and my grin returns.

A Christopher Robin holds out a cup
"I'm sorry, I have no money."
"No, it's for you."
Hot cocoa delivered from the third floor audience.
I wave my thanks to the balcony
An unexpected Gift of Magic
from a child.

HAWK

A new tenant swept off the roof
I'm astonished with her glissando
An updraft causes a temporary teeter
but eight feet from me she circles off to the American flag
Moments later poised alone on red brick
She's unlike other birds in flocks of four
sunglassed against seeing
leaning over the concrete wall,
I gasp my awe and shout,
"A Hawk!"
No one looks up from looking down.
My admiration for the wing tipped reconnoitering
perhaps it was grocery flight,
swoop for a rodent
No, nothing as mundane as dinner,
Rather a sweeping gesture
surveying the concrete canyons
and hearing the call of the poet.

SILVER LINES

Pin Oak leaves fastened tightly to the branches
Staying on when red, gold and burgundy have fallen
Clasping the limbs in leathery bunches
Singing together in a rustle.
On a weedy hillside is the artist's collection of silver foliage
They have escaped the rake's teeth
and hover elevated on the sculptor's tines.
When spring arrives will they be uprooted
Broomed into storage, stacked on canvas awaiting pickup
To be melted down and reincarnated as blossoms?
Nature will rejuvenate by pushing out the rusty marcescence
Replacing the withered with new green
I rely on the ordinary change of seasons.

FEATHER DUSTER CLOUDS

The feather duster clouds
attempt cleaning the noonday moon
off the blue,
but they are ineffectual and are disposed
by the winter wind.
The bits of trash caught in the naked branches
are loosened by the vacuuming gusts
and trail at the heels of a raw boned runner.
He could use the stones from the path
as pocket weights
keeping him from being blown through his workout.
I offer him a shelter of words
where he won't be tossed,
but scientific notions propel him forward.
A body in motion tends to stay in motion
and today I'm not a strong enough outside force.

ELEGY FOR A TREE

When did the saw topple the trunk and its branches?
Was it disease or lighting strike that made the cut necessary?
A nursery is created for the lowly lichen atop the stump
A pedestal for a lively walker to stand atop surveying the spindles
His leather jacketed limbs gesturing toward the twigs
caught up with plastic trash bags.
He insists they are markers of some sort.
They just indicate that the rising creek carried litters of garbage.
Nature uses leftovers to create a triptych on the trunk
Glossy moss grows on the shady side
Butting up a cascading wall hanging of orange fungi
Crowding shelves of chalky stacked plates
folded into a tablecloth of dry rot.
A squirrel is accommodated by a ring of artificial edging
Surrounding the swings of a vacant winter playground.
The twitching tale moves when a squealing child
enters the cafeteria.

VALENTINES

Trio of men Sam and Seth the sons, Dan the Dad
Three related hearts
Different Moms, the siblings share Paternal
Father's evidence in children's grown expressions
Banter and Laughter.

Best friends, Brunette and Blonde
Balancing each other, Rissa and Annabland
Exuberance and Joy
Kyle and Kayla
Did you get together for alliterative names?
Your golden faces made you a matched set.

Sarah and Stephanie separately stopping
Turning around to listen
different weeks, one a biker one a runner
Ernest, Thanking,
Florence says it best, "Kisses to your faces."

I cooked up a Valentine with previous patrons
on the ME-N-U today,
Will YOU be Mine?

DANDELIONS

February Dandelions
Showing your weed beauty yellow in drab winter
peeking out from green barrier construction.
No one picked you to make a braided crown
nor a lover's bouquet for the Saint's celebration
Your showing was
inadequate for extracting wine,
but your hearty blooms establish hope
that the dark and cold will not last
neither will the building site.
The neon safety jacketed workers
will move on with their belts
and landscapers will take over,
but I believe you will find a way
to stand your ground
and burst through any established plan
of turf and flora.

REED, DANNY AND VICTORIA

Lengthy leash, collar hidden under fluffy hair
toasted coconut coat
Chloe is summoned by my voice her mistress is not.
She sits nearly atop my feet
I have no treat to give her, but earnest eyes
implore me to recite
She stays for the entire nineteen lines
still and polite.
"Scientific fact, dogs love poetry."

Always difficult to separate one from the pack
Five male revelers
staggering and cavorting
arms linked bumping
One pulls free and stalls
Apologetic that he has no tip
Assurance, "I read for free."
Supported by the wall, Reed listens.
Stumbling big hug is his thanks.

Straight shinny lacquered brunette and a bill off streaked curls
a couple from a magazine cover
Danny and Victorino
Glossy and Airbrushed
I'm smitten with perfection
Their stance and smile
A billboard for The Beltline

MONTH NAMES

April, first on a February afternoon
Her father named her
A knitted floral cap and mitts without fingers
blossom across her knuckles.
She'll stay swollen warm until spring sloughing.

Janus alludes to beginning, being the eldest of three.
"Why didn't Daddy name me January?"

May, June and Augustus have stopped for verses
Summer and Autumn, but never Spring or Winter
No days of the week have ever introduced themselves,
although there are Tuesdays and Wednesdays out there.
Never have the directions of the compass stopped to listen
Nor have Fire, Air, Water and Earth.
I'm Waiting!

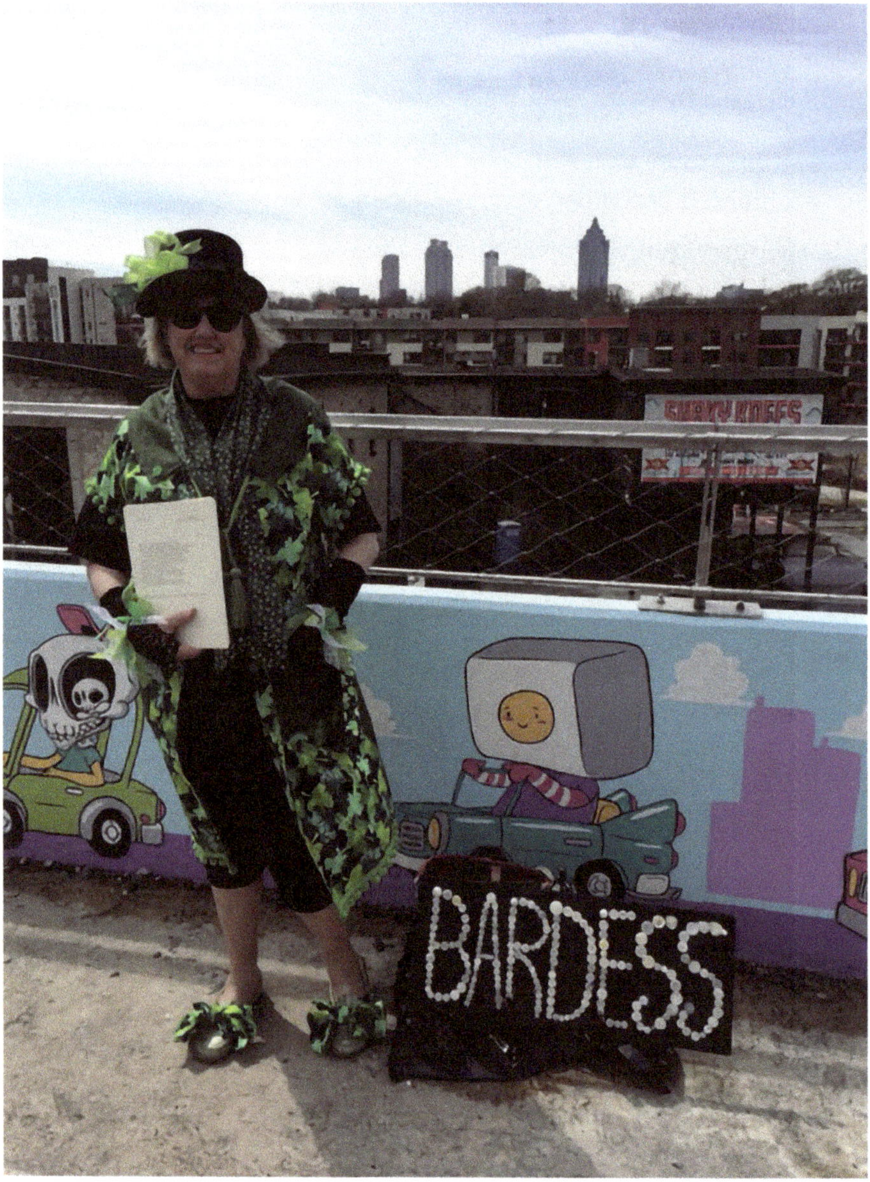
BARDESS

THE ISLAND OF THE SPOKEN WORD

Welcome to the Island of the spoken word
Imagine a mist rolling in
Quill clouds dipping in the sky writing the day as fine
A backdrop of kudzu winding into Celtic knots
No lace curtains, but a colleen,
A Butler serving you green, young emerald lines.
offering gee whiz, Butterflies taste with their feet,
that is why they don't wear socks.
Lucky opportunity to regale while reading
Are you waiting for a certain ryhme,
a rhythm from your past,
a kelly reminder that words link us?
I believe your head tilts and smiles connect us
And
not just on the day when everyone is Irish.

VANDALISM

Nature's hecklers
The crow with its insistent
Caw, Caw cacophony
No lyric of cheerful notes
just a line upon a wire
The growling, barking yipping dogs
trying to exceed their lead
pull around or get ahead.

"Stop and listen and get a free copy."
is my refrain.

A need to be noticed
sophomoric cyclist
"Free coffee, free coffee, free coffee?
I want free coffee!"

I respond emphatically, "Free copy."

A verbal vandaliser,
He continues strident cat calls.
My father said, "Vandalism is perpetrated by
those who cannot create."

MR. PAUL

Robed in a white cotton tee
one small gold hoop adorns his ear
His frequent smiles replete with kindness
Contained gestures contrast with exuberant
words about a bicycle.
The notes of his voice, tempered bells,
round and smooth.
The bike has been ordered.
His excitement is incendiary innocent.
It's glee for life, simple perfect.
I'm looking forward
to his arrival on the fat tire bike.
Presently he extends
a handshake to a young Christian
wearing a Roman legion helmet.
"Pleased to meet you Mr. Paul."
Cyclist enthusiasts both.

TRASH

I'm the archeologist digging for meaning
in the snippets of blown throw-aways.
A gustful flurry pushed pieces of civilization
into my corner.
A deceased lightbulb from a tiny appliance,
an amulet from expired technology.
A neon flag cautioning me of buried optic cable
from an emerging structure.
Someone ate the contents of a cake wrapper
which is now filled with a ragu of brown leaves.
A limp white rubber glove warning me of past toxicity.
An envelope addressed , "To Someone Special"
Handwritten, it is sealed.
I open it.
It is Empty.
I'll fill it with my imagination.

AWKWARD APRIL

Blusters, mechanical and natural
The construction worker's clangs
building overhangs
The wind whipping green parasols of eaves
to protect my face.
The lashes of rain beat the weeds and multicolored clovers.
Where do the bees and butterflies find refuge from the waterfall?
The green pollen and red clay create colored rivers
that will dry up and become ghost arroyos.
All of the winter dust bunnies become sodden
and unable to leave their pebble warrens.
The swollen dirt exposes worm feasts for robins
who are delighted with the opportunity to feed.
April is awkward with its attempts at Spring.

SPIDER OR LADYBUG

Pedipalps touch then taste the children's feet.
Barefooted, the child conquers arachnophobia
climbing atop the cephalothorax, perfecting a balancing act
Arms outstretched, no toppling.
Did the spinnerets weave the metal mesh seat
for the weary parent of the teetering offspring?
Was the man from Milwaukee aware that the series
was benign and could only stain or sticky him with
Sapiens' leftovers?

On second thought,
perhaps it is a ladybug
ready to split its elytra
and fly away home.
But no, the Beltline is afire with offspring,
so alighting here with spotted wings
and Antenna alert
is the place to embrace everyone who is youthful.

MY EXIT

Street lights and neon businesses obscure the night suns
Cell phone screens and keychain flashlights illuminate
six inch circumferences moving through the darkness.
A walker's wrist bands, shoes and striped legs
lit with day glow tape
alert me to his plugged in status.
Bioluminescent fishes flitting through the damp air stream
around me and school together once they are past.
Word murmurings of inarticulate speech move forward
then take a detour
I thought perhaps I could compose a sleepy lyric from
the approaching tune,
but all I am left with are floating shuffles
through the grasses.
I'm alerted by a risen moon revealed
that my exit is next—

WITCHES

Brown cackling magnolia leaf
levitates across the pavement,
climbs a broom of pine needles
and lies in a coven.
A feral cat stalks a cricket.
Summer witches.
Pine cones sodden with water, kicked by pedestrians
cleave to the weeds.
Hairless patches of packed earth
wearing a wig of rolled out sod
are attended by their familiars.
The landscapers whir the grasses with sweeping motions
toothless limbs of Cypress draped with black cloth
waiting to be placed in a row,
the rootball buried with fertilizer.
Some date forward the barrier will expand
replacing the factory made fence.
The groundskeeper will need to shave the needles.
the smell of gasoline,
the noise of motors
controlling the beards of nature,
the whiskers of wild.

READING PLACES

Seven pointed Structure
The Nucleus holds a reader
She's curled up with a book
shaded by the metal
The sun is directly overhead so casts no shadows
My grandmother's nooked window seat
had easy access.
I'd crawl and coil there
shaded from the intensity of sweltering Kansas.

Casey, the dirt eating dog, attended by Charles
wait their turn for the inner circle.
Unlike other perches one must hoist.
I wonder how man and dog will arrive inside.

As a child I was bewildered by shinnying.
I longed to lie in the crook of a tree limb
surveying the lawn below.
As an adult I lied about being a Tomboy
"Remembering" scaling the bark of a great oak.
I imagine sneaking out with a ladder
so I may have access to the Heart of the Beltline Star.

WHITE BUTTERFLY

You alighted in my corner
free from your caterpillar and your cabbage eating
Afternoons.
You stayed to tell me that summer is coming
Your preference for purple, blue and yellow hues
made me wonder why you lingered
flitting in and out
of all the green growth.
I nearly worried for your safety,
but no sparrow nor goldfinch appeared.
The ancients believed that you passed
between this world and the next,
your white wings soulfully
Carrying
the lightest reminder of the longest day
only tiny flecks of darkness on Lepidoptera's
four quadrants.

4TH OF JULY THANK YOU

Encomium poem
symposium gathered listeners,
I salute you with typing fingers,
but without your listening
my words stay on the page.
I drape bunting lines for you
honoring your breeching the gap between us.
Here is a ballad for your efforts to overcome wariness,
praise for stopping,
taking a chance.
Introducing your willingness
sharing your name, a snippet of your past,
a phrase to the future.
I offer you Red, radiant energy
White, mixture of all the frequencies of color
and Blue ribbons.
Thank you for sharing the freedom of speech.

VICTORIA

Victoria who still writes letters every week
does not mention the heat.

"It's almost too hot."
"You should have a tent."
"Why don't you find a shady place?"

Three women who stick to one of the two safe topics
do not stop to listen.
Had they accepted my invitation
Would they have told me about their health?
A remedy for catarrh
a pamphlet listing
fives uses for talcum powder or
the proper way to address a Viscountess

Almost too hot?
I'ii never know what makes it too.

What kind of tent?
An event awning used for her bridal shower
a logo-ed sales pitch protection for cell phones
A garden with overhanging vines.
The only shade offered near are overgrown weeds
where dogs stop for relief.

Victoria leaves with a promise to visit again
No calling card necessary.

PLATO

"Play Dough?
What a great name for a patable Lab
"I didn't remember that it came in black."
"No, Plato, author of The Republic."
Ah, the dreaded dense reading in Philosophy 101.
I took copious notes.

The greatest good is justice, claims the author,
but poets must be banished from his city
encouraging ignoble emotions is our crime.

What is a metropolis without rhyme and cadence?
I don't have dialogues with listeners,
we have conversations,
exchanges about joys and sorrows.
No simultaneous monologues
No strings of rhetorical devices.
My delivery is to excite laughter and smiles
exchanges of memories and names
Hoping that our talking
leads us to know a bit more
unlocking our shared sameness
Extending our hands
Embracing poetry.

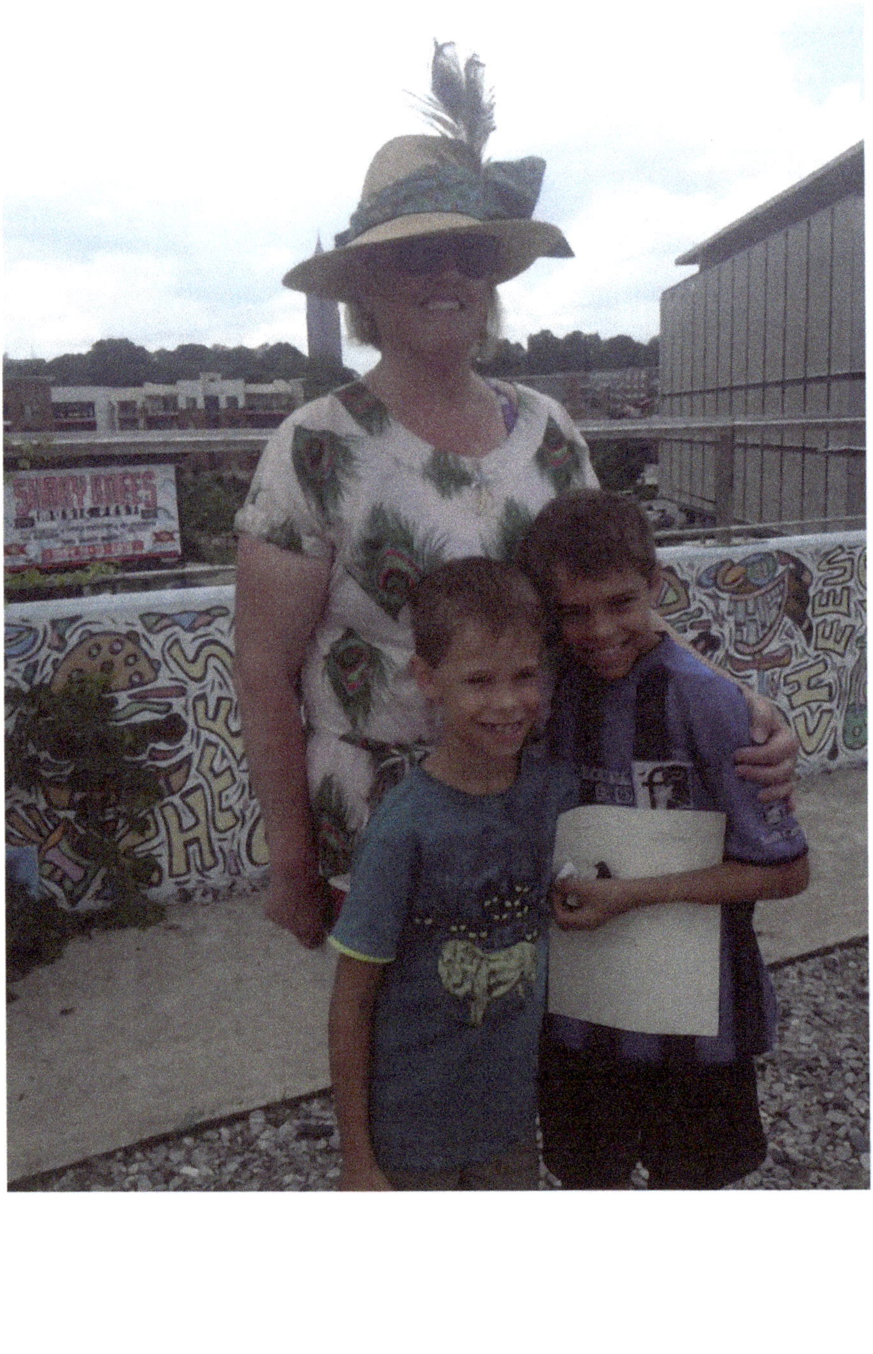

NEAL AND ALEX

Neal and Alex
and now Raine
bringing the out-of-towner Caroliner
They regale me with answers to my questions about vacations
East and West.
I ask for a review of the Chihuly exhibit.
Their comments cause a purchase for myself.
I'll go by car, they went by bicycle.
They are back to school
and I am eager for news of
creatures, critters, colors and equations
They allow a vista of curiosity
for this retired teacher
turned poet.

TRUMPET VINE

The trumpeting vine
reaching thru the honeycomb fence
It trellises itself, Hardy
No wilting, no falling out in July's heat
Unlike the plastic toy soldier who was torn from post
his glue unable to hold him fast.
Like its orchestral counterpart it blasts to be seen
Shouting to bee sniffed
Is it sensed by other species through sight?
Perhaps a glimpse of a darting hummingbird
attracted by its taste
hovering at its opening for the thrill of hot nectar
will be awarded me for my
perseverance in the 95 degrees.

GRACE

Heat and Dust do not deter
Mary from taking a position under my umbrella
listening gratefully to the shade.

Phinezy and Ross
drenched in youthful health
they bring a breeze to the overpass
when expressing poetical enthusiasm.

Alexa and CJ stop for directions
and a photo
I hope I capture them for an urban publication
Her tangerine top
and his fine eyes
make them glossy for Beltline verse,

Grace and Scotty, between them Paige
The twosome students
the visitor betwixt.
Delighted in their stopping
not cautious about Blistering

Of all my listeners this day
Grace is my favorite name.
You honor me, your poise is perfection
and this period you give me
is the time I need to share.

FOUR MONARCHS

Four Monarchs in a hour
flitting to find milkweed
their autumn migration intersecting
with a poet.
This iconic pollinator
foul tasting and poisonous to the birds of prey.
Perhaps they were Viceroys
a different species protected by mimicry
Merrily, fearlessly coasting
through the fall.

Unlike the individual butterflies,
a quartet of thick guys
tromp heavily up the path
their unified cadence
hirsute calves, hairless heads
a formation of flightless Camouflaged
in t-shirts and shorts of varying beiges.
They hug the opposite side of the path
both to and fro
I'm guessing they are not attracted to Poetical nectar.

JOSEPH

Joseph arrives in Atlanta on Tuesday
on Saturday he climbs the stairs to my spot
and smiles in technicolor.
His glorious warmth makes me welcome
The tree that has provided a bit of shade
has been cut
and building mesh has been hung.
Will Kate's tree be toppled when
the market is demolished for the new promenade?
Will one of the last leafy parasols
be closed for steel?
A new listener
is immediate
but nature matures slowly
How many weekends will it take for a planting
to achieve the height and breadth
of Joseph's canopy grin?

SARAH AND NIKKO

Clean, Clear, Pure
In this afternoon stifling
The clarity of her eyes
offers welcome lemonade.
Her coolness is not cold,
but refreshing youth.
Sarah, the lady princess,
not Sadie, Sally nor Tzeitel
there is nothing diminutive about her.

Is this her knight or feudal lord
draped all in black
but deflecting the September heat
with his white flawless epidermis?
His curtain of black satin hair and sunglasses
Starkly contrasting with his powder complexion
Make him a camera study.
Nikko removes the frames to reveal
Almond eyes.

Their beauty combined makes me gasp.
At this moment I wish I had the brushes
of the Pre-Raphaelites
and the perspective of Vermeer.

BRUCE AND ISABEL

Revelers on the Beltline stream past
with popsicles and pups carriages and bicycles
Most ignoring, unaware or waving off,
some respond to beckoning and stop.
Masqued, before words reveal their character.

Jester Bruce asks, "Is the poem any good?"
He listens to the first line
then interrupts.
His Queen Isabel scolds him, "Listen."
He is satisfied and speaks approvingly,
but longs for limericks and puns.
"I offer no profanity."
"No crudity?" he queries
"I serve a plate of word crudités."
"Touché", is his parry
My laugh is my thrust.

Treat for Bruce for Halloween 2016

There was a Jester from Texas
with skewed poetical reflexes
He shot limericks and puns
with his sharpshooter gun
wounding the sonnet's solar plexus

HOPE

Emily wrote it has feathers.
Andy said. "It is good thing, maybe the best thing."

Each Saturday I come with it to the Beltline.
I am prepared to encounter it at least once in two hours.
It's expected
It has never failed,
But I do not wait for it
I call upon it, encourage it.
Not an abstract noun
Concrete as a child
Proven as the energy of exercise
Solid as the restored buildings
Available and on display.

An Action Verb
I am aware of movement
Inhaling as a mantra
An extending continuous exhale
skipping an entrance
hopping an exit
But,
a forever present.

NEAL AND MIKE

Honoring our female relatives we write thank you notes
The polite and civil response for gifts and kindnesses
You have given me ideas, snippets of conversation
introduced new words and phrases
assisted the crossing of generations of listeners:
The Greatest, Boomers, Xers, Ys and Millennials
Encouragement, humor, criticism, disinterest, surprises.

Shy smirks, wide lipped disbelief, tender toothiness pursed sadness
Watching you listen
Your offered and accepted hugs, your praise and shrugs
give enhancements to my lines.
Each week when I depart at 3:00
I feel the open invitation stands for my return.

Here is the card stock heart-written huzzah:
Dear Neal and Mike, a curtsy for your summer heat endurance.
May I enjoy your company in cooler temperatures?

AWE

Let us lavish awe
on unrecorded moments.
The new moon that reduces
every month into a smile shadow
in the clear autumn afternoon.
The blade of green
not caught in the machine
standing alone among the mowed.
The filing stack of leaves
blown into a corner
neatly layered, color coded by the wind.
Vines grown into a winding frame
for a construction site warning.
The film of dust traveling
from a northern forest fire,
A netting of misty debris
grouting lines of the new sod tiles.
Let us leave the numbers of weather reports
to the poetical meteorologists.

DANCER

Wind in the Weeds
Blustering Overture
sending construction sand across my feet and onto my teeth
Grit and Grime
Bring high rise proscenium rope climbing
The dust whirls up under pink tulle of a toddler dancer.
She plies an inner rhythm
Her parents surge ahead
sweeping the cinders out of their sight.
She swans the sidewalk,
her concrete stage
Curtained Mom and Dad have fallen ahead
Leaps of catching up
She exits stage left
They pas de deux, but
She is the principal in today's choreography.

DROUGHT

A drenched leaf blows up
sticks to my pant leg
holds on and gives my brown slacks
a golden print.
Everyone has agreed this week
that we need rain
"Not just a spit or spatter,
No, a through soaking."
Water to settle the disgruntled
bushes and trees which teeter on drought.
The newly laid sod will not survive
the water restrictions
The furrows between the patches
won't fill in to make a carpet.
Without water, the feathered
are found perched on dog dishes
placed by Beltline merchants.
Seeing their reflections
and slashing in the bottled water
poured by a thoughtful pet owner.

JANUS

Janus is two faced
a hesitancy by some to move forward
knowing back-peddling, while possible
on a bicycle is not possible with breath.
You may wear a wrap of the past
being swaddled in the present,
but the future requires unbuttoning the metaphor.
The Beltline is a circle,
but the inlets disappear,
are painted over,
relandscaped, scrapped and draped in new awe-ings
The tracks of Atlanta's alley
are relayed
spiked with trends.
The clay concretes
A landmark disappears
Reconfigured
Parts remain as artifacts
What once was will become new and old

BAD REVIEW

The last step before you stop
planted firm bold before me waiting for the beginning
Shifting from foot to foot, full dress unease
I begin, you wander off, drift afield
Your stance wilts
Your phone rings, you were not committed to the stop.
Curiosity or an insistent companion
incited your hesitancy
I see you squirming friend attempting, cues to you and me.
But now you are quelled and can look down
waiting for this more than 144 characters to end.
It's all right, ok, you're excused.
I would just ask that you do not give me a bad review
just as I would not judge a meatless meal
Poetry is not on everyone's menu.

LYDIA, DEAREST RAY

Lydia, I've met Lydia multiple times
Rhonda has helped and helps me refine my lines
Together they bring others to listen
On their approach and departure they sing my praises
Valentines of Camaraderie
Friendly hearts, busy, off to eat and exercise
I ask "Will you Bee mine?"

Scott on slender black bike stops
His wife likes my poetry but, cannot be here today
He is collecting it for her.
My words form a hug
and I surround him with my physical
I hope that his recitation will emit
Lightness rocking, soothing, easing the Absence.

Dearest Ray is at dress rehearsal each Saturday
He sees me to my stage, making sure props are in place
Returning after final curtain,
asking questions about the matinee audience.
Today you are my flowers and candy,
but everyday my Constant Companion
gifting me with words, delighting with phrases
while providing the complex simplest Love.

Saturday February 11th 2017   Valentine's Day Poem

ANNA

Diamond nosed Anna bike stops to inquire
I am pleased to introduce her to previous patrons
Her chain's links are added to the Saturday cycle
I skip my words across the pavement
expanding reader and listener
The majority of my potential fans
wish to lean over both side fences
to view the work site caverns.
The shake-offs, no thank yous and blank stares
do not put me down
Large numbers do not matter, no polls,
Not a parade to be counted
but individuals to be gathered for the art
of company
A few minutes in your day
Discovery, pleasant
Thomas who admits he was attracted to my scarf,
Thank you for risking the unknown
If you pass this way again and do not tarry
know that you are remembered for that once.

NOON

Noon is not new.
The ancients knew Twelve
not by numbers on a dial,
but by the bright ball overhead.
The circle was their cycle
Birth, growth and Death.
Technology can measure, calculate and dial.
Midnight is marked by science,
but darkness is illuminated
by the half moon's smile.
Storms cannot be interrupted
as the reporting of them can.
Nature may cause a pause in my weekly recitations
but my brain continues to think on you Attention.
You put aside your batteries
to listen to unamplified words
gathered from years of silent reading.
Cranes and bulldozers lift and dig
while jet streams tic-tac-toe the clouds.

FEBRUARY PASSES

A week's touch of summer
which has 100 voices saying,
"Remember the ice storm we had
was it two or three Marches ago?"
Nearly all of the 100 revisit their horror of lost wages and power.
"What happened to February?"
It passed away as it does every twelve months
Its calendar markings with appointments and holidays
are replaced by a longer month
which will be decried as dead very soon.
Mars gives his name to this month
War and agriculture bound together
Nature fighting forward into spring
Winter triumphs in one last battle perhaps but,
fails to win the campaign.

UNPLUGGED SOUNDS

"Did you hear that?"
Last Evening when the rain stumbled
I thought of the pavement unlit and wet
without walkers or cyclists.
I called out to you across the darkness
asking you to listen to unplugged sounds.
The whisperers of nature
the dried up leaf rolling scratching across the stiffened clay
the petals of too soon blossoms murmuring to the ground
the glissando of the night birds' whisking wings
the weeds' tendrils close to overlapping
shushing each others' stalks
The minuscule sounds without interruption
Here are the subtle awakenings
heard without straining, distinct.
Unspoken, unsung by humans,
but still within the spectrum of music and conversation.
We have the pleasure of silence
for these performances
no applause necessary.

APRIL FOOLS

The vain chauntecleer was tricked by a fox.
Is he who lives on the Beltline related?
Chaucer told his tale
He cocks the doodle all day
spreading a hoax of multiple dawns.

Could it be Hilaria, the spring equinox
honoring Cybele making us cheerful and merry?
Let your wheels spin forward awakening.
Smiles widen as the noodles and gobs are played upon.
Be bamboozled by fellows in finely worded t-shirts.
No country marks it as a public holiday
splendid with flowers and banners.
Make a harmless claim that tickles the guileless
Be a Jester cozening the supercilious.

OR

Wave at a stranger with X-panded fingers
letting your fellow traveler know that friendly generosity
is Never Foolish.

TIAR'S INK

Blades of sunshine stripe the bodice
her tresses, strips of variation golden
the bare right shoulder reveals a feather tattoo
She is seated on the spider bench
legs tucked beneath.
What kind of a feather is it?
Is it of a large migratory bird
or is it the Ostrich used for guest book pens?
larger than a quill or a pin
bigger than down
too zoological for an angel's
She rises before I decide to interrupt
her solitude to ask.

Tiar's ink is a Biblical quote
She points it out to me.
She had used the bench as a stretch station
her quilted workout spandex
keeping her toned muscles in hugged grasp.
I marveled at her concentration.
Was she counting?
Mentally chastising myself
I wanted her to be Tiara
the exercising princess of the Beltline
I had rehearsed her coronation
"People often make that mistake,
It's all right."
Noblesse oblige,
I'm forgiven.

HAIR

"Michael?"
"Miguel?"
Grey hair, recumbent bicycle
relaxed on his two wheels
His toes and heels waving
My first hammock to stop
A lounging listener, his recliner
supporting his body.
His ease makes me wish there was room for two
I'd lie next to him and peddle a poem.

Grey steel locks
"Look at me please," I think.
Leo resists my advance by standing sideways
A glance away
I list all of my pluses
he hesitates
I learn that his orange bike is new
and he is thinking of moving to Washington
D.C. or state is my inquiry
"Olympia", one word from his lips.
I cannot keep from saying,
"You have the most magnificent hair!"
"No one has ever told me that."
I think about how the strands would feel.

DYLAN, VIVIAN

Reach into the grey and pull down a clouded shawl
Kneel in pebbles, pick a dandelion for your lapel
Weave the ripe weeds across the way into a carryall
Use nature for comfort, decoration and utility.

Sincerity, Knysna asking earnestly
Scholar, Dylan smiling earnestly
Philosopher, Jay hugging tenderly
Observe youth as your own delighted possibilities
Appoint them your fairy godchildren

John T., proving reasons for courtesy
Po, building stories of dignity
Vivian, attesting to generosity for unrelated guests
Give them places in this present
which was once a theory or hypothesis
now confirmed by their historic spirits
and upheld by you.

CLOUDS

Lightning halberds pierced thru the thunderheads
leaving morning slices piled across the startling Blue.
Our childhood identification game
gives different interpretations.
A stack of serrated knives
Layers of a giant biscuit
Arrows in Diana's quiver
A stretched out den of albino serpents
Bands of grosgrain ribbon laid out in varying lengths
underlining the cyan sky multiple times for emphasis.
But, we all agree on this:
The Great Masters should be out today
Painting.

MAYPOLES

Maypoles with multicolored sashes
held by hands wrapping round ribbons of Maia's waist.
May is the probability that you will stop
You might honor my fervent wish
to listen.
She was the eldest of the Seven
Mountain maiden of the lovely black eyes.
Her place in the Pleiades
established mother of the messenger
Her star is my plea
that you will takes the moments
and not pass me by
But rather
give into the 5th month
and celebrate an interaction of words
with a stranger
who may become an acquaintance.

MOTHER'S DAY

Here we are because of her letting go
She embraced us then pushed us outward toward
Today
Remember who gave you the opportunity

Thank you is one of the first lessons
Use it not just tomorrow, but everyday as a reminder
of your possibility.
Greeting card sentiments are not required
Declare spoken words, your voice
written words, your hand
"I loved, I love, I will love."
These are the chocolates and flowers,
memories of her gift

Say it again!

Hug yourself with her surrounding sound.

For Mother's Day Sunday May 14, 2017

MY PORCH

a quell for quenching parched spirits
Consider this corner a tiny porch,
A cool carousel of sounds
lifting the harsh pavement away
with cascading syllables.
Breezy verbs lilting
drift away stringent heaviness
tilt your sense toward
a respite from heated grounding
alight upon a phrase
be borne aloft in queme*
Give yourself wings for an adjective
and float on springs
Adverbially wafting
for the moment no longer, path-bound.

*pleasure

GRADUATE

Like an elegant egret
the graduate in her 4 inch stilts
leans spindly legged into the canyon.
Her mortar board, white with gold tassels
must be mashed down with her palm
Unlike the bird whose feathers
flutter in the wind but remain attached
Hers decorate only for today
an awkward plume identifying a flight
from 12 years.
The cousin captures her, poised for liftoff.
In her hurried departure she
leaves the grounded walking shoes behind.
I collect them
thinking she may circle back in search
of black-footed sureness for future takeoffs.

JUNE

The 100 watchful eyes of Argus
Juno's security guard slain, but
forever remembered in iridescence.
Her month is rose, breath of honeysuckle
Vitality dripping with pearls.
Moneta, one of her many epithets
garnered attention for another poet, Keats.
She was Sibyl questioning him about the nature of poetry.
Epic Virgil considered her a cruel savage
changing her allegiances capriciously.
For this poet, she is school's out.
The beginning of summer playfulness
seersucker shorts, T-shirts, Roman candles
and the ripening of cherries.

HUGS AND HOLDS

Angles and Arches
Arms in Arms
Branches of fingers outstretched clasping others
Palm against thigh navigating the path
Babies tucked in fronts, heads slumped
A Master of push-ups drops and counts,
leaps up and takes off.
When I extend my words,
A Stopper with radius crossing radius
pats elbows in time to the syllabus beat.
Another uses a fist as a podium for his chin
pondering my lack of rhyme
My physical gestures to your responses
a measured clapping
a cupping of your shoulder
two hands clasping your one
or a hug,
despite your declarations of dampness.

CALDOON

Did your Jaddati or Gidda teach you to listen?
If you're Turkish it was your Nine.
You look at me studying my face
your eyes capture my stare
My words enter your orbit
Comfortable public intimacy
your surrounding listening
making my words symphonic
and I hear Scheherazade's violin.
The pleasure of seeing your orchestral understanding
of the notes of my words.
Dearest Caldoon,
an imaginary asterisk marks the spot where you stand
I'll continue weaving paisley laces
for you to hear.

VIVIAN

This Saturday there are no regulars,
but lines skipped across the sound circle
have drawn Vivian's child asking,
"May I have a copy for Mom, she can't come today?"
Radio lyrics strapped to handle bars whiz by,
but my words get carried
Home.

Shay's shirt declares, "I love Portland."
"Do you?"
"Yes, but not native.
there via Singapore, now here."
He reaches for payment for my poem
"Wow, in San Francisco the listeners pay the poets."
I want to claim Southern hospitality,
but I'm not a native and since when are niceties
Geographic?

Trygve and Jessica introduce themselves
"Not a rare name in Norway, Viking for trustworthy."
In 1995 Jessica was the number one first name for girls.
Hebrew for He sees
They saw me and stopped to hear.

SLEUTHING FOR WORDS

In between my listeners
I sway to the striated clouds
Floating Cirrus notes my inner beats
Hearing words I've wanted to use.
Sleuthing in the Stratus for choices
I am Shamus, my private eyes see
levity and the bits of wispy.

My gaze shifts downward surveying
a caravan of dump trucks descending
White-rusty, Red-pristine, Blue-stained
lined up on the avenue.
Loads of clay are roared off from the underground
the dug up dirt, beds of the subterranean
driven off to be filler.

DOG NAMES

"It's her first birthday."
A white English Sheepdog fresh from the groomers
A pink cardboard conical party hat!
How hot the June pavement must be to her paws.
Fuchsia slippers for her feet
would have been
a better accessory choice.

June Carter strains at her leash,
tugging her owner toward me.
Cody holds her in his arms
while they listen
Bred in Texas as a bird dog
Now, sniffing in Georgia
hunting for poets.

Stephen's black lab
no pooch introduction
"It's been a long time since I stopped."
He shifts the litter bag
so we can shake to reacquaint.
They greet my lines with the same eager smiles.
Steven remains attentive to the last line
but, the canine pulls scentingly away.

HOLLIS

Warm muscular words
contrasting with your serrated edges
your sleek cycle
Not too fast to stop
removing your mouthpiece from your camelback
you speak with angular precision.
I enjoy our discourse
so I admit in a self-chastising tone,
"I know you've told me your name more than once."
Without hesitation, "Hollis."
I am grateful that you do not forgive forgetfulness,
rather, you recognize it.
You wait in slow exhaling time to hear the words
and comment on a line.
In measured moves you mount your bike,
tuck your water in your cheek
and take off.

WE NEED WATER

Rain to enrage growth
the weeds and grasses smother-cover
the silver oak leaves.
"We need water."
The chorus repeats the refrain.
The vines in the corner
wrap around the links, throttling the fence
reaching their tendrils out to touch me.
Their wildness softens the construction signs
uncontrolled curly-cueing finding a niche to expand
while on either side the dust of building swirls.
At some date a landscaper will eliminate
the tenacious un-cowered-by-cranes species
like they did the scrappy seedling that once offered
minuscule shade in my corner but,
beware brick, steel and glass
nature nurtures mutations
which can overcome barbs of chains and chemicals.

TOASTS

Statistically someone will pass this Saturday
who 's marking an anniversary or birthday,
but will they stop to hear a celebration of their date?
I am offering up words on paper plates
frostings of layered phrases
an amalgamation of partying rhythms
for your gravitational pull toward poetry.
What brings you to this passing of moments;
Curiosity, boredom, directions, a break?
Stay with me and receive favors of letters
chosen just for you
Let's make a test to this joyous
cheer that we find.
Our parting gifts?
Knowing the acknowledgement of another.

NEW WORD

Co-ordinated look-smile, wave and voice
all to inspire you to stop.
Behind my glasses you can't see me smiling.
No perfunctory politeness here,
Neither just a glint of generosity
if I wish to change unwilling lips
to let go of a lurking grin.
Perhaps one line will coax the parting and reveal
a row of teeth.
An expansive, "I can't explain it."
Once you have committed to listening,
I'm poet bound to provide:
an unfamiliar word, a brand-spanking new metaphor
or simile.
Perhaps an observation you have missed
that will lead us to a conversation
making a Mobius strip of a new verse
for next week.

LISA AND DIMITRI

Lisa and Dimitri have returned
"How do you spell your names?"
"All with I."
They helped me the last time with pronunciation
of an Arabic word.
Travels have taken them to Lebanon.
Are there cedars on the Beltline?
David's palace, Solomon's temple
and the lining of my Gran's hope chest
all built with the stout conifer.
This evergreen with its aromatic oil and resin
protects wooden structures against insects and fungi.
A call to Trees Atlanta confirms:
Red Cedar (not cedar at all) and Cedrus Deodar
are rooted along the path,
but no Libani with an i.

WORD ARCHAELOGIST

Many of you who stop
leave me with a word or thought
that becomes archived.
I am a practicing word archeologist
who digs through layers of notes
and grey matter clippings to retrieve
the gems and treasures of our encounters.
A casual remark becomes the subject of poetry.
Your pre-frontal cortex gives you
social proficiency to interact with me.
In turn, my temporal lobe seeks word recognition
to provide a weekly joy for me to share.
Both you and I rely on our visual-occipital
when next we meet.

WHAT MIGHT HAVE BEEN WRITTEN

Her thrifty smile is flashed quickly
She wants directions, not poetry.
I am frequently asked to be a tour guide
or reference point.
If I have the knowledge, I oblige.
I am unfamiliar with her destination,
so she leaps off leaving me in mid-word.
"Wouldn't you like dot, dot, dot?"
Had she stayed perhaps we would have
hit on a point of mutual contemplation,
a word, a sighful moment, a laugh or
perhaps she missed a chance to be named
at a later date in a series of lines.
I did not miss the opportunity
to ruminate over
what might have been written.

WHAT'S NEXT

Summer may be giving up.
Fall is trying to erase the sun's strokes
by giving the Green autumn fire hues.
The heat surrenders to a warmer clime
The Crisp that we missed
is just weeks away
Our anticipation is not noted by nature
the seasons will change when they do
without our permission or beggary

How soon will fickle humans be pleading for spring?

We long for nature's upgrades
The seasonal assembly of adornments
a simple weed glaciered with ice
or sprinkled with dust
limpid with rain or broken with dryness.
Without nature's directives,
we lose our senses in the pervasive
consistency of technology.

TEACHERS

Two Mobs of students
Moveable lectures
Herded by the pointing instructors
shouting over the triad of cranes

One keeps the trainees on toe
all the while rejecting my spiel
"They don't have time to listen!"
Did I mistake his snarl?
Was I a distraction
to his canned rehearsed lines?
"Architecture is Art, embrace a poem
to round out the equation of engineering."
He bats the air toward me
and tightens his leash.

The other strains to hear and steps closer,
cupping his charges toward me.
The ones at the back stay
in the middle, one parts two others to move forward
A couple of slouched relaxers
smile and mmm along
"Hey that's great," a couple of unisons.
One initiates applause
Some finger-snap me and accept my offering.
"Can I take your picture?"
"Yes, you May."

JAKE THE DOG

Renaissance circus dogs
easily available and trainable
wore ruffs or Elizabethan collars
Kelly and Todd carry
Jake, A Chinese Crested, rescued dog.
His tuffs of hair on tail and neck
contrast with his hairless freckled torso.
A steel pin in his leg impedes his mobility
His frail carriage causes
concerning comments from Neal and Mike.
He will be a UPS truck for Halloween.
He won't be delivering anything but smiles
in his costume.
Surely a delivery truck van doesn't wear a leash.
For what does a dog trick or treat?

GRACE, NOT MIRANDA

Still life
bicycle leaning against bench
rider seated and reading
facing my corner not the path
I eye her as she turns pages
and finishes her coffee
She is engaged in her lines not mine
I miscalculate her rising.
She moves toward the
discarded plastic among the weeds.
"I glanced up, it bothers me to see it."
She gathers up the ribbed containers
and moves deliberately to dispose of them.
Upon her return we discuss
Trash and Shakespeare.
Othello is her favorite and she
understands Iago's motivations.
I don't
I wished to iambic pentameter her,
but her name is Grace, not Miranda.

GLEN

Seldom seen accessories, parasol and fan
useful on an unseasonably warm November afternoon
Marie offers a draft of air
I decline, I've learned to forecast
my perch's barometric pressure
and dress accordingly.
Glen's tropical shirt and straw fedora
adjust his temperature
creating a jaunty gentleman.
Weather, then food
popular topics of conversation.
I'm traveling to colder climes
and always
Lusting after the perfect cannoli
I get directions which include
Our Lady of Pompei Church
in Greenwich Village.
Glen's green penned directions get me there
I'm glad to be home,
but you were right
confectionary bliss.

PENUMBRA

The penumbra of predawn
then daubs of pastel unmoving in the sky
the morning star, a period to the night.
A black bird sweeps across the pink
landing alone without a note.
This bit of a silent film's title sequence
Precisely, never the same.
Shadows and luminesces
I hold up my word kaleidoscope
only able to capture a sideways glance
of the infinite combinations and permutations
that nature provides at any moment.
Add humanity
film speed is increased
and I must call out to One or Two
refocusing my view
Initiating a slower pace
recitation for your focused faces.

GG

G G in concert with daughter and two grands
Her presence is out of context.
She is acting Mistress of Ceremonies
making introductions all around
and announcing her pleasure at finding me
with a Huge Hug.
Granddaughter asks if she may hug me too.

A man and his retinue, six children and two adults
circle round after his announcement,
"She's a poet, it says so on the sign."
I sense nonplussed
as I hold each chia's palm
Seemingly bewildered by the man's enthusiasm.
A memory of my dad stoping at every
"Something Happened Here " sign
as we drove East
"It's historical!"
They thank me dutifully polite,
but each wants a copy despite the admonishment,
"We only need one per family."
Each gets one and I wish I had a red ribbon
to tie around their rolled up document.

BIRD BUILDERS

The high-rises surround my perch,
but the buildings of a small bird's nest is nature's
reminder that twigs and grasses make effective domiciles.
Even in December these minute builders
gather their supplies, flying them onto the site.
Each piece laid in a time honored instinct.
When the building behind me is complete
will there still be a place for these winged architects
to create homes?
Will the next generation immigrate
to a less congested avenue of the Beltline
taking their sweet silent flit with them?
The beatings of their wings,
an inaudible metronome
for my weekly rhythm and rhyme
will be missed if they depart.

MANHOLE COVERS

Manhole covers trap the falling dogwood blossoms
Molded sticky metal, gluey with wet pollen.
The green grunge of pine tree paste
adheres to the streets and windowsills.
An orange caution cone marks a hole
The cover is nowhere in sight.
Who is down there?
Did the worker take the lid
to be a gladiator shielding against
Urban legend alligators and anacondas?
Abandoned exotic pets, living under the street
Tunnel dwellers, unafraid of the dark
Lying in wait at the bottom of the slick metal rungs
I'll stay above ground with my imagination.

SMALL GIFTS

Mozart's Magnum Opus, his Requiem
Charlotte's was her egg sac
This is my holiday opuscule
Small gifts, Large thoughts
word offerings for my listeners
You bring pleasant reminders
of my purpose on the overpass
The wire-dangled construction worker
who acknowledges me with a bob of his head
The generous smiles of individuals
who do not break their stride
A tiny wave of a toddler whose parents
do not wander over to hear
my rehearsed thankfulness.
The I-know-not-which breed dog
straining at his leash to lead
his master to me.
He sits on my feet and listens.
The cyclist racing by, but raising
a gloved hand in salute to my presence.
Let this be my lagniappe to your
traversing the Beltline.

DONNA

Donna's Expansive hug
in the frozen afternoon
She is elated to see me
"I'm so glad you're here!"
I don't use exclamation points,
but she deserves two!!
Her friendliness convinces
me we've met.
She listens ebulliently,
her eyes expressing excited wonderment.
I am momentarily saddened
that I do not remember this expansive spirit.
How could I have forgotten
an introduction to this woman
who exudes Joy?
Like the Lady of the Home,
you came to my hearth and made the sun shine warmer.
I am pleased you stopped to include me
in your aura.

CELLULAR LISTENERS

A murmuration of sunglass clad
mimicking each other
with clicking phones
They find this communal roost
and pose and pose
repeating the stance.
Flocking omnivores
no untidy nesting
just sleek black with glints of green
silk and fleece
Posting on the rail
no clinging to the wire
they are cellular

LORI

Lori dresses in smiles
each one pleased by something different.
The curled corners of her father's cooking
the diminutive bow of self reflection
the open mouthed, "Oh my Gosh"
as we share a commonality.
The upturned ribbon
delicately accessorizing her brunette sheen.
Her job is to make sure all the extras
are dressed historically proper and
appropriate for the scene's weather.
She did not spot
the awkward coral raincoat, tiny printed capris
and orange patent booted mannequin
walking up the path.
I know she would remove
the offending garment with
an unbuttoning twist of her lips
"You need to change,
here, put this on."

ATOMS OF THANKS

What is beforehand if belated is after the fact?
My four chambers send out pre-flourishes of words
to my listeners named and unnamed
to long time enthusiasts and newly initiated.
The science of the left gives my lungs air to breathe
so that I may expel my thoughts for you.
The right atria and ventricle supply the whole body
with element number eight.
How easy it is to dismiss oxygen as dull and inert.
Fact: most reactive of the non-metallic elements.
So, forget gifts of Silver, Gold and Titanium
on the loving holiday
Instead, air your kindest thought of caring
giving atoms of thanks,
molecules of appreciation
and equations of amour
to those long known and perhaps
just met.

WORMS — ROBIN HEAVEN

Robin heaven, the warm rain brings forth
a feast of fat worms.
Will the birds indulge in a midnight repast,
Can they see in the dark?
Their utensil beaks lifting the snakes
gelatinous offering for their offspring
for me, it is avoiding
stepping on the gushy specimens that
the flooding has unearthed
Reminding me of hooking worms for fishing
wriggling to tantalize the trout
and the 8th grade biology dissection formaldehyded
into rubber.
Are there feather-tailed that prefer the dehydrated
jerky version that are still in the afternoon sun?

MATTHEW AND TIM

Matthew and Tim
Men of civil gentility
Introduction making
no cacophony accompanying them
Manners from a previous era
no bluster, no braggadocio
passing pleasantries and inquiries
of each other's family members.
I always am reminded to ask after Matthew's mother.
Salon on the Beltline
They greet other listeners
with questions that begin conversations
about shared interests.
Afternoon tea without sandwiches and tarts,
but instead savory stories
and sweet intervals.

MORPHING REALITY

Phantasmagoric Beltline
The past behind me with a grist mill
that has survived the wrecking ball.
In front, hidden by a dragon and a mural train are
railroad ties soon to be transmogrified into a walkway
entrance to the future.
I access my perch by elevator
which was once a dirt path carved
by determined hikers.
The stones in front of my pedestal worn through time,
a prehistoric ridge
now marked by spray paint signs delineating
something's coming.
The complex succession of weekly changes
seeming somehow fantastical, but I know
they aren't a pre-spring imagining
rather an ever morphing reality.

DAYLIGHT SAVINGS TIME

The day light was saved this week
so that we might enjoy more hours of Apollo.
Without the sometimes intemperate rays,
The green would be drab blistered brown
or pale colorless unnatural nature.
Today we celebrate the virescent glory
between the optimism of yellow
and the insightfulness of blue.
Lucky me, to be here with you
who stop to hear my metered tales.
Proud that you share your strides
with this versifier.
Thank you for pausing on the 17th
to muse a moment with a merry minstrel.

(To: Lou who is not a fan of alliteration)

VOLLEYBALL KEN

There is a cyclist peering over the net onto North Avenue
Many stop to look out
at the Vista but...
when I ask them to listen
they wave me off
turn away
ignore or don't hear me.
I speak first.
"wouldn't you like to hear the poem about the Beltline?"
"I've ridden by many times
decided to stop today."
Plays non-competitive volleyball
with a bunch of guys for fun.
"FUN, emphatically emphasized, where's the joy?"
Ken must be the Setter,
the playmaker, blocking and serving.
My serve is off the path.
I've spiked suggestions to move closer
and use a megaphone.
I'm the Poet Libero
the specialist, making the game exciting
keeping the ball of meter alive,
Challenging the sports metaphor.

MOTHERS AND CHILDREN

A camel, double backpack
I thought they carried their water in the hhumps.
This one has two fisted bottles of neon liquid.
Clumping hurrying to kneel down in the shade
behind a high dune.
A Ox, multiple shopping bags in each hand
trudging to a baby shower
laden-lumbering toward an unfamiliar address
hoping to arrive on time
at the gated compound.
A kangaroo with a swaddled roo
a diaper draped over its face,
keeping the sun from scorching the tender flesh.
Behind the mother, a Joey dawdles
with a melting popsicle, dripping and dripping…

STOP AND HEAR ROSES

Extricate yourself from the mob
Swim against the current
with your hands out and make your way to me.
Slow down, back up
when you hear my voice,
turn around.
Come to me, I'm willing and wanting
and waiting to make you an enjoyer
of rhyme and reason.
Break from the crowd
I'll provide cadence
and capture for the moment
a piece of peace with you
No Worldly words,
but a flow of the sonorous
a tide that does not rip your seemingly
hurried Saturday rather,
slows you for a crawl,
a whispered walk
Stop and hear the roses.

REPURPOSED MATERIALS

A piece of uncollected art
has attracted two species of birds
striped tails strip away the blowing plastic.
Will it be used like the blue tarps
protecting roof from rain
or will it be used for reinforcement
for the nesting walls?
Many artists repurpose materials
I'm supposing that this was a dry cleaners coverup
and a discarded mirror frame.
I never met the artist
No signature on the work
But I'm sure
She would find pleasure to know
that a couple of resourceful fellas
have found somewhere to hang the work.

ROME

I thought of you as I walked the ancient Streets,
pondered the burning of both cities.
What remains there
Remains here
Layers of rock before man
This piedmont, rich with
igneous and metamorphic
has crumbled to red,
No structures, nor humans can claim
the ages of rock formations
Our erosion is measured in years
not eons or periods
We demolish, tear down, rebuild
But, after our time is done here
The Rocks will be somewhat
more worn, but present
for a sequel

NOISES

Time approaches in every direction
on wrists, afar heard bells,
ambulances racing past,
passerby, "Catch you later."
Will it happen when they catch a falling star?
Every increment is accounted for.
Is there a moment for nothing?
an uncaged, unbuckled time
with unmarked unmonitored heartbeat?
No appointment for blinking eyes
No chimes indicating timelessness
The pace between thoughts.
Wasted?
No, relished longing for repeat,
but no schedule, scheduled
just surprised
barely discern-able
after the sigh
un-noted, in the furrow of the brow.

FARMERS AND POETS

Relying on the weather
not just rhyming about it
The rhythm of the rain
is poetical beat
but, I have been poured out.
No one wants a soggy manuscript
Hot topics for poems melt in summer heat
crunch beneath my feet
when ice slips the path
Unable to deliver my produce to market
I bring the pulp home in my tote
keeping it for distribution in the coming week
Farmers and Poets
both hopeful
mindful of the seasons.

UNNAMED

As each wheel rotates,
the physics that keeps you balanced
is taken for granted.
Which spoke number is yours?
You are a pedal pusher,
you have control of the cycle
rearing up on your alloy bronco
you look back.
I urged you to turn around
you feigned disinterest
but I noticed a glimmer,
your slight hesitation.
Did you ask yourself,
"Who is she?"
or was my presence
a reminder of something you neglected to do?
I continue poeming your story
until someone stops to listen.
You are not unsung,
just an unnamed wheelie.

DAN

He applauded with his eyes and voice
his optical and vocal expressiveness
contrasted with the stillness of his limbs
His gentle musculature hung on taut bone
Linear
His lean against the fence,
a balanced algebraic equation
Both sets of fingers, integers
perfect Ten.
 a straight line and a circle.
Software engineer speaking with me
Breaking down my code,
extrapolating evidence that science
and art are not at odds.
Dan's lines on a screen
exchanged and changed by others
riffs of squiggles and dots.
the shortest distance between
two points of view
is a conversation.
His coda, "Maybe I'll stop again."

A SLEEVE OF POEM #133

Tattoos:
Wallace Stephens' Light Spider
Frost's Stopping
Thomas' Raging
Poe's Raving
Literary inking
Rather than printing to paper
they festoon the skin
with poetic lines
I never imagined that a listener
would commit my words to his body
but,
one promised
when he exclaimed
that #133 expressed exactly how he felt
I suggested a limit of the first and last lines
"No, all down my arm.
A sleeve of words.
Is that ok?"
"As long as you give me credit
and return to show me."
Perhaps he reconsidered
the length, cost
and commitment to an unknown
But,
I'm still flattered by the mention.

BRIDE AND GROOM

The silver assent with an uphill river
a perfect aisle for Bride and Groom
a bicycle between them
Or
They could ride the elevator
emerging on the sidewalk
empty water bottles attached to the rear wheel
of their tandem.
She could ride side seat
so her lovely gown won't be spoke-caught
His patent shoes slipped into toe cages,
He will stand and pedal for two.
They moved away last year
So…
They won't be stopping good-bye
so that I may confetti them with
word showers.

BEING BITTEN

Concrete will converge with stones
connecting new towers to the path
wooden troughs hold cement until
curb hardened
Walls where once were weeds
Rise sculpturally from piles
replacing the utilitarian chain links
Keeping passers from falling
or jumping.
The water that collects
in the construction site lakes
gives life to the mosquitoes
who lite upon my neck
as a congregating space
Whining
while we converse.
I have forgotten my Mace
against attack,
So,
I leave this week
reminded that nature does not respect art.

DOGS AS ASSISTANTS

Calling cards are presented
A letter of introduction produced.
Dogs forgo the societal rules;
straining collars to sniff out
new acquaintances.
The well bred willingly greet the mutts.
Their barks, shouts of recognition,
rub-againsts, handshakes of
"It's been a long while,
but I remember you."

Stella pulls up in front
She has just missed John Wayne
but his scent remains.
She entwines Giana's slim ankles
with her black leash
Stella's antics, a starter
for a conversation with Lori
who has been standing by.
They delve into their related fields
I wish to offer much appreciation to
the four legged assistant
for launching an interest between
a column of printed silk
and shorts and t-shirt.

SWALLOWTAIL

A swallowtail alights on
an orange banner of construction tape.
Why has this ribbon been looped through the links?
It is alone.
No others on the expanse of fence.
Does it mark an important spot?
Is it a point from a blueprint?
If I removed it,
would a catastrophe occur?

"Meet me at the spider bench."
It's no longer seated there.
Three Acts close
other sets are built.
I've blocked my entrances and exits.
First behind the olde Sears Building,
Then City Hall East
Now Ponce City Market
I'm still North Avenue overpass
But,
when will it be renamed?
Perhaps Longitude and Latitude
are needed to find my location.
Would you carry a compass?
What degree would you go to find me?

SPY NOVEL

I'm a recorder
a listener
but these two spy dressed guys
aren't talking to each other
They are addressing their phones.
Dark glasses hide eyes and intentions
They are together aren't they?
"Check it out, Check it out."
"I know this guy, I'm telling you."
"I'm telling you, I'm telling you."
"You can so like hide everything else."
"A squeegee sensor, so be it."
"I'm on it, I'm on it."
They point their phones at each other.
Will they shoot?
I'm a witness
as is the black lab leashed to the fence
waiting for its owner.
I haven't been called to testify
Perhaps the plot fell apart.

#2 PENCIL

A yellow number two pencil
Chinese graphite encased in the color
of royalty and respect
Now common and discarded
The ferrule which held
the gum eraser is gone.
The pink pumice
with the new school year smell is missing.
If I take it home,
It will need to be sharpened.
I'll use my father's pocket knife
but the incense of sawdust
will be absent, instead
little fingernails of cedar shards
will fleck my desk.
I'll need a Big Chief tablet to practice
the Capital and formally minuscule B and b.

AUTUMN

Autumn is announced by an Equinox,
the first heated gasp of Fall.
Hot breath blown across brittle leaves
not colorful rake-fulls,
rather leathery broken ribs
wheezing as they tumble.
I catch one underfoot
it cracks, boiling water on ice.
Remember when the tomb was discovered?
The clutch of flowers left for a Pharaoh
became dust disintegrated when touched.
Which mourner placed them there?
No card with condolences,
nor hieroglyphics
indicating who lost.
Did the archaeologist brush the bouquet dust
into a bag
and tag it with a poem?

GECKO

Two green glossy lines
one inverted
entwined on a pole
dance moves of the gecko.
The other laid out flat on a silver pipe
His autotomy is evident.
Did he self-sever?
Was his tail like a pair of Velcro stripper pants?
Did he shed to escape?
Unlike the canyoneering climber
who cut off his arm to survive
this lizard's appendage will grow back.
Both are still in the sunlight
only
licking their eyelids to keep them moist.
No brows blocking out the kicked up dust.

O'CLOCK TIME

"I've been friended by 401 people."
The verbing of the Nouns.
I am "acquainted with" perhaps would be better wording.
When did counting friends become equated with your emotional income?
"I was unfriended by my best friend."
"Oh my goodness."
Meeting new listeners every week
Face to Face, O'Clock time
Inquiries lead to people we have in common
Corrina photos with Chuck
Ben was taught by Suzy.

Hearing your sighs
joining your giggles
asking for a hugg
that's with two GGs
to comment on the heat and cold
to eschew politics and religion
to share a respite with a someone
who is a stranger no more.
Small incidents of polite civility
tipping our hats to each other
Pleasantry.

MY THEATER

Cake Batter Clouds
Egg whites folded gently
No fear of a rising storm
I will stand clear today,
just cool sun
lighting my readings
The crisp edges of walls
hold my lectern in place.
My self appointed space has remained constant
among the changing sets and scenery.
I've been Rained, Iced and Heated out,
but never sold out.
You have come from:
Out of Country
Out of State
Out of Suburb
attending numbered performances
without tickets
Not knowing the topic,
but crossing the apron of stones
to listen.
I bow to you.

OCTOBERFEST

"Roll out the Barrel"
wafting from across the park
Were there bosom laced punk Heidis in attendance?
I couldn't smell the wursts
nor blow the foam from atop the steins
Only the muted sounds of the crowd
and refrains from the accordion.
I gasp.
Direct from Central Casting for Octoberfest in Atlanta.
Technicolor embroidered.
"Come over here, Stop."
I wave him to me,
Insistingly, "Please" emphatically.
"You're my first suede lederhosen walker."
Young, muscular, airbrushed
Virile (I've never used that word),
J.P.,
Nothing like the shorted portly players in Oom-pah bands.

ROBYNE AND CLIFF

Horizontal and vertical stripes
Blue and white integrated into Cliff's shirt.
His attire as defined as his Queen's English.
Sibilant praise for my poem
Gracefully thanking me for my contribution of artful lines.
His companion, Robyne, lithe and elegant.
He entreats her to come see me every Saturday
Until my last stanza.
She promises to be his emissary,
Ambassador to the Beltline,
to collect the last nine.
I silently syllogize a platonic
Shakespearian friendship
Horatio and Hamlet, both were male
The union of truth, the closeness of wisdom.
J.K. Rowling gives us this century's
Hermione and Harry
This is a white rose offering to Robyne and Cliff.

UNTOWARD

Words come and go
leave pages that were welcoming
now abused, overused.
A deluge of acronyms and jargon.
I want to diligently search,
then find the letters in combinations
I'm looking for.
It is possible to discover the word
buried beneath.
My hand poised waiting in position
for the conducting brain.
When it hides I type ( )
leaving a space for it.
Often, I notice a word I wish to use,
but have no poem for.
Today, I used untoward correctly
in a conversation.
I clapped, proud I had succeeded
with the nearly archaic.

LEAVE-TAKING

Leave-taking
nature's finished with this year's leaves.
Five cycles of seasons
Two hour Saturdays I've jumped in the piles of words
choosing them for connotations
and culled connections.
(Today I'm tied with Mr. Shakespeare)
Next week I'll buckle the Belt
completing the circular journey with you
At some distant date when the path is finished,
perhaps you will have a mental mileage marker
remembering where I once stood.
Sharing 310 hours
with the loyal listeners,
and the one timers
Perhaps you never stopped
but wondered in passing,
who was the hatted woman
with her simple sign?

ADIEU

"i get it, You're like channeling Ginsberg."
I think, am I howling a counter culture?
Surely not, Beat Generation obscene.
Neither abbreviated Twitter text,
nor double vowel ejaculated
combining, creating, jarring hateful words.
Breath lengths, not hurled "aganist the harsh wall of America",
but pitched teasingly onto the Beltline.

"Is Dickinson your favorite?"
Exposed on an overpass
not reclusive in a white clapboard house
Neither Amherst Belle nor Atlanta borne
Eccentricities of beauty I sing.
The tune with words
Perching you in/on lines to be somebodies.

Whitman restrained by the multitudes and himself.
Egocentric electric body songs of Walt
Self-promoting, Self-Publishing
Mass praise for the group,
Nearly 3 million square miles
My 22 linear miles
citing odes of individuals each Saturday.

Walt, Emily and Alan broke poetical conventions
penning through the eras
You sang your songs to me
and I recorded and played them back
Looping 155 strands, Lovingly
around my fair city
The Bardess gently bids,
Adieu.

Lee Butler retired after teaching English for 22 years. Over time, she has worn many hats – including the ones she designs and sells – and explored multiple venues for artistic expression. In her latest such endeavor, she creates characters and designs and sews their costumes for competition at DragonCon, the world's largest cosplaying convention.

The inspiration for this collection of poems in your hands came when her husband introduced Lee to the Beltline, a 22-mile loop path encircling Atlanta, Georgia that retraces a former railway corridor. She quickly became enamored of the site, and paid tribute to it by spending two hours each Saturday reciting a new poem about the Beltline's people, natural beauty, artwork and architecture and rewarding people who stopped to listen with a copy of the poem on card stock.

Her goal was to one-up the Bard – which she did – by completing 155 poems about the Beltline, or one more than the number of sonnets that Shakespeare wrote. She considers these poems, in this volume, as her Love Letters to her city. Now, Lee is working on her next book of poetry, about her grandmother and mother – Hazel and Faye – both of them, like Lee, former English teachers and seamstresses.

Printed in the USA
CPSIA information can be obtained
at www.ICGtesting.com
JSHW010250211024
71944JS00007B/22

9 781957 184630